Small Things Count

🦋 Simple Ways to Live Christ's Love Each Day

To Francis,
    Keep those social-justice
wings fluttering!
                    Sincerely,
                    Jackie O'Donnell
                        1/16/10

Small Things Count

Simple Ways to Live Christ's Love Each Day

Jackie O'Donnell

SMALL THINGS COUNT

ISBN 978-1-926625-23-2

Printed in the United States of America

FOR MY HUSBAND, FRANK
AND OUR SON, BRIAN
—TWO GOOD MEN.

"Do small things with great love." – Mother Teresa of Calcutta

❧ Contents

❧ *Introduction*
Christian Butterflies

"The Spirit of the Lord is upon me, because He has anointed me to bring glad tidings to the poor. He has sent me to proclaim liberty to the captives and recovery of sight to the blind, to let the oppressed go free, and to proclaim a year acceptable to the Lord" (Luke 4:18-19).

You are one of many people who want to help make a better world, to take the love Jesus freely gives us and pass it on to those who need it most. You already give to charities but still feel a need to do something more "hands-on." Due to time or personal constraints, you can't go on marches or vigils or participate in big public actions. What else can you do?

True Christian concern lies in our hearts and is shown by the little things we can (and should) do daily that reflect our love for all of God's family. It can be as simple as a word here, a visit there, some reading, or just an open-minded conversation.

Yes, such uncomplicated acts can have world-changing consequences. Meteorologists talk about the 'butterfly effect.' Essentially, this is the theory that a butterfly flapping its wings, say, in San Jose, California, can affect the weather in Bayonne, New Jersey, or even in Hong Kong. Others have applied this theory to human behavior. In other words, the tiny action of one small creature—or of one lone human being—has the potential to affect the whole world.

This book will show you how to be a butterfly. It is your resource for specific little things you can do as you live your everyday life. By the end, you will know that, when it comes to answering God's call to help care for all His Creation, small things really DO count!

❧ *Chapter One*
First, Understand Your Purpose

"Do to others whatever you would have them do to you. This is the law and the prophets" (Matthew 7:12).

Y ou are ready to change the world. But before you choose how you will go about that, review some basic attitudes and why they are important. Understand what it is you are about to undertake.

Some Definitions

We often hear the terms *social justice* and *charity*. Many people, not clear about what they mean, are uncomfortable with these terms and unsure of how they fit into the life of a typical Christian. The following definitions should help.

- *Social Justice* works toward a society which promotes just relationships, safeguards human rights, helps those in need, opposes oppressive laws, and maintains the dignity of human life.

- *Charity* is related to *Social Justice* in that it is aid given to those in need; meanwhile, social justice works to correct the basic causes of the injustices that have led to the need for charity.

Most Christian denominations have agreed that there are certain positive ways of thinking and behaving which, when cultivated, can help us live as Jesus taught us, thus building a more socially just world. In essence, these are attitudes on which we base our actions as we live not in isolation but as part of society, part of God's family. We call them the 'We-Attitudes,' because forming a better world for everyone is something we must do together.

Below is a list of these "We-Attitudes." Don't worry if they seem to overlap. They aren't totally distinct from each other, nor are they all-encompassing. However, for the purposes of the butterfly-experience you are about to embark on, they will give you some focus.

The "We-Attitudes"

- We reflect God's image.

- We nurture God's family.

- We are our brother's keepers.

- We empower our brothers and sisters.

- We honor our brother's and sister's labor.

- We recognize God's family throughout the world.

- We protect the earthly home God gave us.

- We accept God's gift of peace.

Now What?

Does this seem like an impossible task? It really isn't, if you take little steps to improve the corner of the world you live in. All you need is the willingness to observe, to try small, new things, and to keep an open heart.

Turn the page and start to adopt these attitudes, living each day as Christ intended.

🦋 *Chapter Two*
We Empower Our Brothers and Sisters

"Blessed are the poor...hungry...weeping..." (Luke 6:20-21).

First, Think About It

Y ou know that old saying, "God helps those who help themselves?" There's an element of truth in it. The hitch is that a person struggling on his own, with nobody helping him, is doomed to probable failure. Where's God in this? Simple. He's in us. He helps that person by sending *us* to stand with our struggling brother.

We support him through our efforts to bring about more just laws and institutions. We encourage him by letting him know we care about his future. We increase his confidence by expressing a changed attitude. We give him hope by involving ourselves.

That involvement comes in many forms. The following pages offer some examples.

English Practice
You have an ability you probably don't recognize as a potentially

valuable gift to someone else, your ability to speak English. It's something you can easily and freely give to a friend or co-worker who is struggling with the language.

Without a command of English, people are often judged as foreigners, outsiders, or unintelligent. This decreases their chances for jobs or promotions and makes them targets for prejudice. To help, all you need do is to talk with your friend often—at lunch, at break, at the park while your kids play on the swings, whenever you can spend a small block of time. Offer him or her this chance, not as a teacher but as someone to practice a difficult language with within a comfortable setting. To make it more interesting, ask if you can learn some words and phrases in your friend's native language. Eventually, you can hear all about the new opportunities and increased respect he/she's earning just because you helped break the language barrier.

Shop For Causes

Your anniversary or Valentine's Day is almost here and you don't have a gift for your Special Person. Why not choose a gift that says, "Let's share our love!"

Present Sweetie with something that benefits a group or cause. Many companies dedicate proceeds from the sale of certain products to fighting cancer, preventing domestic violence, supporting teen programs, or helping victims of disasters such as the tsunami in Southeast Asia. Others offer Fair Trade products (not the same as *Free* Trade), like food items whose production has been overseen to ensure that workers have not been enslaved or mistreated. Possible gifts include cosmetics, gloves, scarves, tee shirts, fitness aids (exercise mats, heart-rate monitor watch, etc.), lunch boxes, coffee, and chocolate.

Watch for items that say "I love you" not only to your loved one but also to vulnerable members of God's family.

[See "How to Shop for Causes" in Appendix A1 for an idea of products offered, how to make sure the profits go to the cause advertise, and how to guard against charity scams.]

Be Heard!

Politicians don't have a clue! They don't care about injustices caused by the death penalty or Patriot Act. It's okay to try kids as adults and then throw them into adult prisons to harden and learn new criminal skills. Homeless, elderly, disabled people–all that matters is money, not lives and human dignity. Or so it sometimes seems.

If an issue strikes a moral chord with us, God expects us to exert our influence. A simple way is to contact those in power. Send a letter or email. Call them (the phone book lists legislators and their contact information in the government section). Remember, too, that our representatives read newspapers, so write a letter to the editor. According to Congressional staffers, constituent calls and letters are the top two most effective forms of communication with legislators.

If you get a positive response, write your newspaper's Action Line and encourage others to express their opinions. On the other hand, if an elected representative won't listen, wait awhile, because soon you can vote in someone who will.

Write A Letter That Your Lawmaker Will Read

1. **Know the specific name and address of the person you wish to write.** If you aren't sure who your Senator or Congressman is, you can find out by going to the United States Government Offices page of the phone book. There you'll find the addresses of both their local and Washington offices, as well as their phone numbers. Or go to www.house.gov, enter your zip code, and you'll get the name of your representative and District number.

2. **Show respect.** Address both the letter and envelope using his or her proper title. The "To" portion at the top of the letter and the envelope should use this form of address: The Honorable Margot McGlintey, followed by the address. The salutation should be "Dear Senator [or Congresswoman] McGlintey."

3. **Before starting to write, decide on the <u>one</u> specific point you want to make.** This letter is no time to empty the garbage can, dumping all your disagreements on your lawmaker. To be effective, the letter must concern one issue only, and if that issue has many parts, one major idea within that issue. For example, don't try to settle the entire energy debate but just try to get her to see the benefits or folly of one certain energy source, like wind.

4. **Keep the letter to a maximum of one page.** That's all most people read, anyway, and you're writing to a very busy office. The letters that the staff read through and pass on to their boss will be the ones that are short and to the point.

5. **Be logical, yet human.** A ranting, emotional letter will lose any force it might have had. But a mere recounting of facts and figures, which he probably already has at hand, is just as unconvincing, because it doesn't have your personality in it. Clearly state your opinion and why you feel that way, without complaining, whining, or blaming the President, a political party, or anyone else who might be considered a scapegoat.

6. **Identify yourself as a constituent**. After all, you're writing to someone who is expected to be responsive to the people in her own district. Be aware that your recipient has time to listen only to constituents.

7. **Include a personal touch.** The most effective letters are those which tell how the writer is personally affected by the situation or proposed law being addressed. Be specific about what this means to you and why.

8. **Type the letter, if possible, or write legibly.** Typing isn't vital. However, the easier to read a letter is, the more likely it is to be read and considered. Most readers have

an   unconscious negative reaction to writing that is hard to read, and that reaction can run from just impatience all the way to an impression that the writer is not worth listening to because he is sloppy or unintelligent.

9. **Send it on time.** If there is legislation pending, make sure the letter arrives *before* the bill is voted on. Otherwise, it's too late.

10. **End the letter with your full name.** If you type it, leave a space between *Sincerely* and the typed name, then sign in that space.

Finding A Job
"I can't find a job anywhere!"

All of us know people who are unemployed or underemployed, as well as the frustration of not being able to help. Now there is something we can do, and it takes only a few minutes. We can tell them about the free classes and support groups that help people find jobs. They are held in our own and in many nearby communities, at churches, community centers, schools, even at companies. They're advertised at these places and usually have open enrollment so that people can drop in anytime. Watch for these announcements and keep an ear open for them around your work or church.

Rather than commiserating with your jobless friend, suggest that you help him find one of these classes or groups. Offer to drive him there if he needs transportation. After he has attended a session, talk to him about it, encourage him, steer him away from negative feelings. It may take a few sessions before he regains hope. Together, look forward to the time he happily waves his first paycheck at you and you share a celebratory hug.

Homelessness
Look at that homeless bum! How could he choose such a life?

This common gut-reaction comes from not knowing what actually puts people on the streets. In October of 2005, the Association of Bay Area Governments (California) cited four major causes of homelessness: chronic drug/alcohol abuse (33%), serious mental illness (22%), domestic violence (18%), and youth under age 18 (14%). In other words, people get caught up in circumstances they can't control and didn't set out to be in.

No, we can't magically solve the complex problem of homelessness, but we can change our own mind-set. From our new perspective grows not only a different way of talking to others about the problem, thus changing their attitudes, too, but also a new way of treating homeless people we encounter. (Warning: it will be harder to ignore them.)

When you feel the Spirit, contact an organization dealing with any of the root causes cited above and, with others who have had an "attitude transplant," work toward reuniting our homeless brothers and sisters with the rest of God's family.

Don't Just Stand There!

I'm so scared. I heard that guy tell the pharmacist he's 19. Guess I look older than 12, 'cuz he smiled at me. At first I thought he was kinda cute. But I don't know him, so he shouldn't have rubbed my back. He's touching me some more now and is saying bad things to me. I yelled, "Stop it! Leave me alone!" Now my 6-year-old sister is crying. I'm yelling louder. People are all around me, but nobody's doing anything. Why won't they help? There are lots of people, lots of adults. Won't they do something? They're just standing there. I feel so alone.

(This actually happened in March 2006 in a supermarket pharmacy. No one helped the girls. Their father, worried that they were gone so long, went to the store to check on them. He was the one who finally confronted the store's manager and was the one who called police. Why him?)

Hotlines

He holds a sign saying "Hungry." She comes to work with a bruise, for the second time this month. His limited English hinders his search for work. Her tears won't stop as she thinks about her husband, dying of cancer.

Help is out there, but people need to know how to get to it. You can provide the roadmap. Carry a list of hotline numbers. The list should start with "2-1-1," if it's available in your area, which offers referrals in various languages for food, shelter, senior services, addictions, counseling, and other needs. It should then list several toll-free numbers that offer help for child- or elder-abuse, addictions, suicide/ depression, runaway youth, domestic violence, and families facing grave illness. Give a list to people in crisis, not pointing to any specific number except "2-1-1," and let them choose either to talk with you or to just keep the list to empower them when they're ready to get help.

If the moment is right, offer your cell phone and some privacy for the call. It may take just your one unobtrusive act to save a life.

[See "Hotlines" in Appendix A2 for list of toll-free numbers.]

Mircroloan: The Perfect Gift

Looking for a novel birthday or Christmas gift? How about a pig farm in Bolivia? This is how it works: you buy a gift certificate for as little as $25 from www.kiva.org. The person you give it to goes to that site to choose a recipient for his microloan. That money, combined with other microloans, will start or expand a small business in a developing country, allowing people there to earn a living, educate their children, and generally improve their families' lives. Kiva loans don't earn interest but to date 99.72% of the loans have been repaid.

A similar site is www.microplace.com, an e-Bay subsidiary begun in October of 2007. They require a minimum of $100 investment but promise a 3% annual return. They don't offer gift certificates yet, but you could make up one of your own for, say, a grandchild and go online with him to set up the account in his name. Together you can watch a small investment change people's lives in a big way, and the grandchild can boast, "I own a jewelry store in India!"

Beat The System — Volunteer

Ever think the System is out to get you? For those who society prefers to ignore it's not paranoia but actual sad reality.

23

We can change their lives, though, just by working with groups dedicated to their well-being. Yes, I'm talking about volunteering. But not for far-flung causes like Save the Whimzit. Make it something close to your own heart. Do you have a family member who has a special challenge? Then be part of a project like Special Olympics, which helps mentally and physically fragile people participate in society. If you had (or were) a troubled teen, become a Foster Parent or Child Advocate. Maybe the elderly are close to your heart. If so, Catholic Charities has an Ombudsman Program which needs volunteers to investigate complaints and advocate for elders.

Your church can tell you about other volunteer opportunities that hold personal meaning for you. Focus on a group of vulnerable people and offer a few hours to improve their lives. You'll be helping people in distress, and you'll be changing the system that put them there.

On Christ's Team

One of the least-loving places we visit is where our child's team competes. Be it soccer or softball, you've sat in the stands, cringing when a parent cusses at the referee or some adult encourages fighting or intentional injury either directly or indirectly by non-verbal approval when it happens. This can be an opportunity for you to be a good example to your child, the teams, and the adults who aren't acting like part of God's family.

There are many things you can do. Ask that man not to use ethnic slurs around your kids. Find something during the game to compliment the small, awkward child on the team. If your own child acts with violence, make sure your language (body and verbal) clearly indicates your disapproval. In front of other adults and the team, express your appreciation to the referee for his time and fairness. When you leave, have your child help you dispose of your family's trash, plus what was left by people around you. Keep your eyes, ears, and heart open; you'll find ways to live your beliefs.

❧ *Chapter Three*
We Honor Our Brothers and Sisters Labor

"When the Jews persecuted Jesus for healing a man on the Sabbath, He answered, 'My Father is at work until now, so I am at work'" (John 5:17).

First, Think About It

When we introduce ourselves, we are frequently asked what we do. Of course, we're being asked not about our gardening or golf but about our work. That's because so many of us identify ourselves with what we do for a living. We take pride in it or, if we're unhappy, we look for another job that will give us satisfaction and dignity.

In our society, there are unspoken beliefs that some jobs are more important than others and that some are low-class or demeaning. It's important to notice that this attitude does <u>not</u> normally come from the person who is unemployed, underemployed, or suffering under unreasonable job conditions.

What can be done to ensure the rights of workers and the dignity of work? It starts with how we treat the workers we meet every day. It moves into actions we can take that are small but can have the impact of a successful march on the legislature.

The aim of the activities in this section is to remind us to show our conviction that work has nobility and that workers have earned our respect. It's so easy to do if we just take advantage of the opportunities we stumble onto each day.

Servers

Ahhh. Work's done. Tummy's happy. It was a hectic day but your simple meal out finally let you relax. The food was so-so, but you didn't have to cook! That young server was very patient when you sent back your cold food to heat up and when she brought a rag and a smile to clean up Joey's spilled milk.

Here's a chance to recognize the "We-Attitude" of honoring our brother's and sister's labor. Show your appreciation for good service: tip more than the expected minimum; compliment the server; tell the manager how pleased you are; fill out that comment card, being sure to mention the server by name; as you leave, tell her you hope you get her table next time. Most of us speak up when something goes wrong in a restaurant, so why not say something to let this person know that we value her *and* her hard work?

Day Workers

What a mess! The weather's getting nicer but there are far too many repairs and clean-up chores to be done. What to do!

Help yourself and the poor while fostering the attitude of honoring labor by hiring a day-worker from a local day-worker center in your community. They are often run by church-affiliated groups who screen workers and match their skills with the jobs you need done. You pay a reasonable wage, probably around $10 an hour, and the center sends you people who are qualified to do the job you need done.

When not out on a job, these people spend their time in training, improving their English and gaining skills that make them better workers for you while building a brighter future for themselves and their families.

So, what's to lose, except for that broken fence or that peeling paint or the hopelessness that these willing workers have felt in the past?

Fair Trade

Try some guilt-free chocolate. The pounds may stay but not the regrets about how that yummy stuff got to us. Do the same with coffee, tea, rice, sugar, juice, honey, wine, flowers, crafts–all sorts of things that frequently reach our homes through the mistreatment of workers in other countries. In places around the globe many people, often young children, work under harsh conditions to support their families. But it's the only work available.

The *Fair Trade Movement* aims to change this, to provide employment, fair wages, decent conditions, and money that goes back into their communities for health and education. This is not *Free Trade*, which is political, among nations, but *Fair Trade*, protecting the well-being of people. Participate by buying products on-line (Google "Fair Trade") or at Safeway, Trader Joe's, Whole Foods, Cost Plus, Peet's, Starbucks, and elsewhere. Watch for the Fair Trade symbol on packages. Ask the manager. Make your interest known. Then, maybe just one more chocolaty nibble wouldn't hurt.

Hotel Workers

What a nice hotel room. I'll just relax. No bed-making. Ahhh....

Enjoy, but ease the lives of the people who make your stay possible, the hotel workers. Their job-injuries occur twice as often as for others in the service industry and are far more serious. They must meet a room quota, despite faulty equipment and under-stocked supplies. Already shorthanded, they aren't allotted extra time for rooms with luxuries like in-room exercise equipment or a pillow-top mattress (100+ pounds) and its linens (16 pounds). Most injuries come from strong cleaning agents and repetitive motions. Because these women need their jobs and are very proud of their profession, the industry takes advantage of them.

We can help by being on their side. Take the "Hospitality and Human Dignity Pledge" on the next page. Consciously decide what you are willing to do and check off those items. Sign the form and tuck it away where you can review it from time to time. Stick a copy in your suitcase for when you travel, just as a reminder. Get started now doing what you said you'd do. And next vacation, when you see the person who cleaned your room, don't forget to give her a smile and a warm "thank you."

Hospitality and Human Dignity Pledge

I recognize that the requests of hotel services workers are reasonable for all workers: livable wages; paid sick days; affordable family health coverage; a voice on the job; humane and safe workloads; and protections for immigrant workers. I pledge to support them in their quest for these rights by doing the following:

___ Tell friends about their struggle

___ Write letters to hotels asking for more humane working conditions for workers

___ Pray for workers at home and in my congregation

___ Call, write, or email corporate management when workers face harassment or intimidation

___ Stand in public support of workers (sign petitions, attend events)

___ Make workers aware of my support by talking with them, letting them know that they matter

___ Be careful not to leave a hotel room in such disarray as to add unnecessarily to their burden

(signed)	(dated)

Burger Boy

I wish they wouldn't treat me like that. I know I'm just a kid. And my

English ain't too good. But I try. I don't like how people look at me, like I ain't worth much. I don't wanna be here. Nobody else will hire a kid who don't know much yet.

I see my parents struggle. I can't ask them to give me no money for fun or school or nothin' and I see how sometimes they don't eat unless I bring some burgers home that woulda gone into the garbage anyways. They both say don't take no handouts unless you at death's door. We been there twice I remember.

I'm gonna finish school. Go to college. Get a real job. Make it so they don't have to worry no more. Then, when I go to Hamburger Haven, I'll tip the guy and give him a high-five, 'cuz I know why he's there.

Invisible Workers

It's magic! Mail appears and trash disappears. Somehow the electric company knows how much power I use each month. After gatherings, the church grounds become clean overnight. Fresh vegetables are abundant at the market. A taco just shows up at the drive-through window or a choice of goodies in the cafeteria cases. Funny, I didn't see anyone do a thing.

It was all done by the Invisible People—workers we take for granted because they always do their jobs. This year, celebrate Labor Day each and every day. Make it a point to watch for the person who delivers mail, reads meters, picks up trash, prepares food in the cafeteria, or hands over that taco. Be aware of the individual caring for your church grounds. Notice the human being who tends the store's vegetables. In other words, recognize the *workers*. Make a special effort to thank them. Let them know that you appreciate the part they play in making your life easier. Feel free to shock them with a word of praise or gratitude. They deserve it.

Picket Lines

There's a picket line. What should you do? Lower your head and push past to get your quick quart of milk or go elsewhere and avoid the situation entirely? Neither! Practicing the "We-Attitudes" includes honoring the rights of workers. That means you should not cross that picket line, at least until you've taken the time to understand their side of the story.

Talk to them. Read their literature with an open mind. Follow both sides of the issues in the newspaper. Remember that picketers are real people who have a right to be heard and to have the work they do respected and justly compensated. Then let your conscience be your guide. If you truly believe their position is wrong, shop there, knowing that you've given them the courtesy of listening to them and fairly considering what they have to say. On the other hand, if you believe in their position, show your support by shopping elsewhere and letting the business know why you're doing so.

Workplace Bully

Does someone at work love to make people around him miserable? If you feel that way, most likely you aren't alone. The Workplace Bully never heard of, nor does he care about, the dignity all workers are entitled to.

Confront him, not with a solid punch to the jaw but with a calm request for him to be more reasonable. Tell him plainly that he makes you feel uncomfortable or humiliated. Explain why specific demands he makes on you are excessive. If you do this in front of others, you minimize the chance of verbal warfare and, at the same time, embolden co-workers who have been suffering silently. Join with them in a sort of support group, one that doesn't feed each other's anger but keeps you from feeling isolated and helps you find ways to counteract the bully's actions that don't turn you into a bully. Soon your lagging self-respect will return. Together you'll make your job site the fulfilling, safe environment you deserve to work in.

They've Got It Made!

"They've got it made!" We've all said this as we watch people doing their jobs. We're convinced they're overpaid for what they do. Are they? Teachers have short days and long vacations (when do they do lesson plans and grade papers?). Garbage men ride around all day and do nothing but pick up trash (what health hazards do they face?). Cops sit around eating donuts and are never there when you need them (except when they are and put themselves in harm's way for us).

Next time you hear yourself saying, "They've got it made," assign yourself the task of finding out about their job: salary and benefits; required education and training, both original and ongoing; hours and duties expected from those hours; health and safety issues the job poses; job security; and working conditions.

Jesus called on a variety of workers, from fisherman to tax collector to tent-maker. We should remember His lesson, that we must respect all work and value the worker. After all, we labor in a pretty big vineyard.

Jesus and Home Repairs

If Jesus owned a house that needed repairs, what would He do? With His training in carpentry, He'd do some of the work Himself. Still, He's very busy, what with watching over the world and all, and could use some help. Would He, like many of us, do what our society encourages us to do?

Social norms support our looking for a DEAL. So, we hire the people who charge the least, suspecting that this job means much-needed food for the family or this month's rent. We take a "don't ask/don't tell" stance regarding licensing and legal status. We don't question the wages or working conditions the contractor provides for those he hires. We may even separate ourselves, watching to be sure we're getting our money's worth but not offering the workers a snack, water, or use of a restroom. Before they disappear from our lives, we may forget to give a kind word or a tip for work well done. After all, they were paid to do a job for us; it's not as though we'll ever see them again.

Now, back to the original question: What would Jesus do?

❧ *Chapter Four*
We Are Our Brother's Keeper

"My heart is moved with pity for the crowd, for they have been with me now for three days and have nothing to eat. I do not want to send them away hungry, for fear they may collapse on the way" (Matthew 15:32).

First, Think About It

Sometimes being part of our community's family means helping out financially. Everyone needs to eat. Everyone needs housing and medical care. In short, no one can survive without having some very basic needs met.

In this economy, many people are unable to do this for themselves. People have debilitating illnesses, are laid off from work, experience tragedy and loss in their lives—all through no fault of their own. What has happened to them could have happened to us. It still might. The fact that it hasn't so far gives us a responsibility to help.

Not all the needed help costs us a lot of money. The most important aid would be to see that laws are passed to protect these people and take away the conditions that caused their current position in life. Other ways to help improve people's lives entail our rethinking how we go about things we normally do. The following pages give some ideas to try.

Warning: some of them are actually fun!

Electronics

Spring is traditional cleanup time. Confronting you is the corner of the garage with those electronic gadgets your spouse says *must go*! Guess that means a run to the dump, although those items are poison to the environment.

Stop! There are alternatives. You *can* put your old electronics to better use than polluting the landfill. Give cell phones and laser or ink-jet cartridges to the Fraternal Order of Eagles, which supports children's and veterans' programs with them. Give a cell phone to a battered woman, a disabled man, or an elderly couple, showing them how to keep it charged and how to dial the free emergency number without having to sign up with a cell phone provider. Also, the YMCA gives refurbished phones to domestic violence shelters and victims and to the elderly and disabled. Watch for recycling events for electronics often held as fundraisers for a church or organization and plan to drop off your old microwave, television, VCR, radio, keyboard, or copy/fax machine.

The options are there. Mother Earth will thank you and so will the vulnerable people you help.

Disposing of Electronics: Some Helpful Hints

Computers

- Before donating computers, make sure to delete all your files, and clean your hard drive by using disk-cleaning software to wipe out all information. Free programs are available at www.shareware.com.

- The National Cristina Foundation (www.cristina.org) will match you with groups that need old hardware to provide job training for the disabled.

• Donate computer monitor, TVs, laptop computers to HOPE for Retarded Children, which sells to an authorized state recycler. Drop off at a HOPE center or call them for a pickup of multiple items.

• Check with local Knights of Columbus, fraternal organizations, and schools to see if they have a recycling program for electronics.

• Look in your newspaper's local events calendar for "E-Waste Collection."

TV Sets: The very old ones contain cathode-ray tubes that contain toxic lead. Call the local sanitation or environmental department to find out when electronic waste is collected or check out the Basel Action Network's list of responsible recyclers near you (www.ban.org/pledge/locations).

Cell phones

• Most senior centers take them for distribution to seniors for emergency use.

• Collective Good (www.collectivegood.com) takes your phone and in return makes a donation to the charity of your choice from a list of 350.

Rotating Shelters

Change lives fifteen people at a time. That's the opportunity some churches have, as they host the people in something like Silicon Valley's (California) InnVision Rotating Housing Program. Such programs, available in many communities, house a group of men for several weeks in their church hall or gym, offering them food, shelter, and transportation to job training and interviews. The group rotates to another church after awhile and receives the same hospitality while they work toward getting back on their feet. Is your pastor aware of such a program in your community?

Maybe you personally don't have the energy to set up such a program. Once you've found one, though, you can easily help support it. For example, cash in on sales on bottled water and soft drinks and give some to the guests to put into the lunches they carry to their training sessions and job interviews. Gather all those little shampoo bottles and soaps you've brought home from hotels and give them to these men for their personal grooming. Like to bake? Make a batch of cookies, brownies, or muffins to sweeten up the three meals a day provided for them. Or help with those meals. You can be part of this great program that fosters almost all of the "We-Attitudes" at once.

Share A Hobby

How can you make a more socially just world? Enjoy your hobby.

We are called to help others. We give money to charities but we can also personalize and humanize our help. Someone who knits or sews for relaxation can make items for a specific charity (new handmade items are a treat). When you cook your specialty, double up and take the extra to someone who is sick or living alone. Bake your favorite cookies, muffins, or scones to take to a homeless shelter or center for battered women. Do you go to the movies often? Brighten the life of someone on limited income by treating him sometime, explaining that you'll enjoy it more in his company. Do you enjoy gardening? Help an elderly or disabled person plant a small, manageable garden at her home and then stop by often to admire its progress. If you unwind by doing auto repairs, volunteer to help get that laid-off neighbor's car into running order. The key is this: figure out what you do as a hobby and then share. You'll find it more enjoyable— and more fulfilling—than ever before.

Room For God

I've always known that in my busy life I need to make room for God. What I'd never thought about before was making a room for God. Recently, though, two of my friends from church told me about their special rooms. Both are wonderful ideas and support many of the "We-Attitudes."

One family has a *God Room*. It's a spare bedroom set aside for whoever God sends. It has helped, among others, a couple get over an economic hump, keeping them safe and off the streets, and a youngster whose parents had given up on her. When people leave, the family waits prayerfully for the next person God sends their way.

My other friend has a *Peace Room*. Her living room, done in calming tones, is set aside for quiet and contemplation. No arguments are allowed in there whether by family or visitors.

Sound impossible? No. Both situations work well and my friends report untold blessings as a result. What better place to listen to God and abide by His will than in our own homes?

Safety First!
Christian teachings tell us that everyone has the *right* to a safe environment plus the *responsibility* of helping provide one for others. Home maintenance lists abound that tell what should be done each month. But what if you know someone physically incapable of doing those chores? How can you help?

You can check locks on his windows, doors, and gates and make sure they work properly. You can test her fire, smoke, break-in, and medical emergency systems and put in new batteries. Or replace burned-out light bulbs (house, porch, outside security light) and frayed electrical cords. Move those flammable items from around the water heater, furnace, gas range, or anywhere else there's a flame. Get together with another person to clean debris from the clothes dryer vent, which is a big, often-overlooked fire hazard.

Look over the following checklist. It lists basic tasks that take only a little of your time but mean greater safety and security for someone you know. Go through your own home and mention to your elderly or disabled neighbor that you wouldn't mind checking out her home while you're at it. It's the neighborly (and Christian) thing to do.

Jackie O'Donnell

Safety Check List

Do Yearly

- Clean rain gutters

- Note setting on water meter. Turn off water main for an hour. Check meter again to see if the gauge has moved. If so, there's a leak somewhere that needs attention.

- Check water heater. Inspect for leaks and flush.

- If stove has a hood, give it a good cleaning and replace filters.

- Check locks on windows, doors and gates. Make sure they work properly and all screws are tight.

- Clean or, if needed, replace furnace filter.

Do Twice a Year

- Clean lint from vent in clothes dryer (from dryer drum to where the air is vented outdoors).

- Test emergency (fire, break-in, medical) system, if one is installed.

- Replace batteries on smoke detector. Hint: write date of replacement in indelible ink on the battery.

Do Monthly

- Test smoke, heat, and gas detectors, plus fire extinguishers.

- Remove anything flammable near water heater, furnace, gas range, or anywhere else where there's a flame.

- Check for frayed electrical cords.

- Clean garbage disposal by grinding up two trays of ice cubes made from 1 cup white vinegar and 1 gallon water.

- Replace burned-out light bulbs in house, on porch, and outside security light.

Food Fast

Kids rock! Every year, at churches all over the country, teens and young adults confront the problem of hunger by participating in a "Food Fast." They learn and pray, all while existing only on juice for 24 hours (a real challenge for teens). Then they apply what they've learned to an outreach activity, like making sack lunches and taking them, along with some conversation, to homeless individuals at a local park.

This is something that we could all do, each in our own family. Another option is participating in Operation Rice Bowl, a yearly Lenten activity at many churches, in which money that would have been spent on skipped meals is gathered by a family then donated to an organization fighting hunger. Or working at places like a local soup kitchen or food bank, where we see both the problem and the human beings who are affected by it.

It doesn't matter *what* we do, so long as we do *something* to educate ourselves about the problem. Then, armed with what we've learned and the empathy God has blessed us with, we must work to erase the causes of hunger, a condition that affects 20 million adults and 13 million children in America.

Protecting Patients

Please...I'm here... Somebody.... I know you're visiting your father in the next room, but I've called out a dozen times for a nurse to bring me a blanket. You must have heard. Please get someone for me. Last week I was so thirsty, but nobody would answer my call button, and the woman visiting her friend in the other bed became irritated with me and closed the curtain between us. This morning I heard the laughing again. One aide was mimicking my slurred speech, the other was calling out my daughter's

Jackie O'Donnell

name like I do when I really get feeling downhearted. I'm old, but I'm not deaf or stupid. I've been in this place for so many months that I'm less than a piece of furniture to them. If you tell someone in charge and wait to be sure something is done, then I'd be so grateful. No, it won't get you in trouble, but chances are, nobody will even think about treating your dad the way they're treating me. Please... somebody....Please.

Closed-wallet Giving

Everyone has one or two hours. True, we may have to steal them from a television program or that yard work that should be done. On the other hand, it *is* okay to reprioritize every once in awhile.

Let those two hours make a difference. Hand out shampoo and food at fairs held for the homeless in your community. Give blood through the Red Cross or a local hospital. Work toward wiping out a disease and, meanwhile, care for the sick, by distributing contribution envelopes to neighbors for the Cancer Society or Heart Association. Serve a meal at a soup kitchen during a non-holiday season, when volunteers are scarce. Shop for newborn items to give to the church's layette program. Pick up people without transportation and bring them to church, grocery shopping, an appointment, or to vote. Use your imagination. You'll figure out other ways to help people in need. It could be called 'Closed-Wallet Giving." What it is, though, is "Open-Hearted Giving"—giving of yourself.

Teach Charity

Sondra, a friend from church, decided when her children were very young that they needed to learn charity. She taught them to give something to every person who asked. Each time they were approached by the disabled vet outside Longs Drugs, the homeless man on Market Street, the uniformed woman from Food for the Hungry, the Salvation Army man with the Christmas kettle, or anyone else asking for help, they would give a little something.

I asked, "What if the person's a fake or will spend the dollar on alcohol or drugs?" Her answer was another question: "What if they really do spend it on food for themselves or their family?"

This woman was teaching her children an important fact. That is, it's our job to be charitable; it's God's job to decide who He sends our way and why.

Charity on a Budget

Yes, you'd love to give more, but what can you do on such a tight budget? The answer is, always keep others in mind.

Use coupons and set aside the savings until you have, say, $20 to donate to a charity. Recycle often, keeping the money in a baggie in your purse, then give what you have to the next homeless person you meet. Watch for good 2-for-1 sales and donate that second box of cereal or sack of flour to a food bank, the church food pantry or collection, or a family you know who needs it. If you go to garage sales, pick up clothing and household items in good condition to give to a shelter for battered women or an organization helping disaster victims. Cashing in on a great sale on yarn? Get extra and make items for layette programs sponsored by many churches.

We don't need to be rich to make a difference; we just need to watch for opportunities to help make life better for others.

Chapter Five
We Nurture God's Family

"I give you a new commandment: love one another. As I have loved you, so you also should love one another. This is how all will know that you are my disciples, if you have love for one another" (John 13:34-35).

First, Think About It

Very few of us are hermits. Most of us are nourished by being part of a family and a larger community. Our membership dues include watching out for each other, helping whenever and however we can. We try to strengthen our group, alleviating the suffering of its members and protecting them from harm. Just as we don't allow our children to go hungry or be in danger, so we shouldn't tolerate such conditions for our larger family, our community.

Usually, this simply means reaching out to people, not with a dollar stuck into a coffee can but with a heart and a hand. It starts with observing people around us. We'll see a need, then recognize in ourselves an attitude we hadn't noticed before. Sometimes that attitude needs an adjustment.

That's what the activities that follow are intended to do—teach us ways in which we can get involved, truly becoming part of our community-family.

Reconcile

We are called to be family, yet we let family squabbles divide us. Any time is the perfect time to heal a rift, to reexamine our relationship with someone we've harbored bad feelings for. It could be a relative or someone at school, work, or a group we belong to. Maybe I don't even remember exactly *why* I feel wronged. But I remember the person doing something cruel or hurtful. Was there a misunderstanding? Has one of us changed? To find out, I must be the one to take that first step. I'll pick up the phone, or write a note, or speak to that co-worker, or talk to the person I've been avoiding at church. For I know that through reconciliation with God He embraces us, and with each act of reconciliation we make in His family, we embrace God.

Include a Loaner

Wave a palm of welcome! Well, maybe you shouldn't go *that* far. But just as Jesus, a stranger, was welcomed on the first Palm Sunday, you can greet someone who feels like an outsider any week. There's the man who hugs the corner during church service, the young couple in the back trying to manage their small children, the widow who comes faithfully each week, the person you've never seen before. They come alone and they leave alone, untouched by the family that is Church.

It's past time to let them know we welcome them. We can sit or stand by a newcomer or loaner or invite her to sit with us. We can invite him to coffee and donuts in the church hall. We can easily engage people in conversation by commenting on their cute child or an upcoming church event. They just need to feel noticed, and we need to let them know we consider them part of our caring, Christ-centered family.

Healthy Marriages

AFTER the kids are grown and we retire, THEN we'll have time for us! Most couples think this from time to time, putting their relationship last on their priority list. Wouldn't it be better if our kids grew up with a different outlook, one that says that Marriage, as the heart of Family, is important enough to nourish?

We can do this in our own homes and among friends. Find out about Marriage Encounter weekends and couples activities groups like Encore Amour, for people who have remarried. Do a date-night exchange, taking turns watching the kids while one couple goes out on a date—or just goes back home alone for a few hours. Give that extra set of tickets to friends who need a night out. Or take their kids with yours to the Children's Discovery Museum and turn over your pool or hot tub to the parents for an afternoon. All these things are inexpensive or free to you but priceless to your friends. Your reward comes when they return the favor, and God's community benefits from healthier marriages and healthier families.

[For information on Marriage Encounter, go to www.wwme.org.]

Write A Prisoner
You did the crime, now do the time! We've all heard this. Paul probably heard it, too, when he was jailed for his faith, although most people today are in prison for *un*holy acts. We call prisons "Correctional" and "Vocational" institutions. We say we want people to learn their lesson, get out, and sin no more. Meanwhile, they're hardened by a solitary, harsh life made worse by friends and family who forget about them. Our faith calls us to consider all members of our Community, to support and embrace all members of God's Family.

You can minister to imprisoned brothers and sisters simply by writing them, giving them a positive stake in the world they'll be rejoining. A little afraid? We have some simple guidelines to make writing a prisoner safe and comfortable for you. Remember: you're not out to change their lives, just to support their efforts in changing their own.

[See Appendix A3 for instructions on finding a prisoner to write and a guide for corresponding in a safe, comfortable way.]

Safe Haven
"Children Welcome Here." That's a sign you might hang on your front door. Living the "We-Attitudes" means protecting our children. In this

45

economy, though, many are latchkey kids or home alone because their single parent has to run to the store. If your heart is open enough and your temperament calm enough, you can provide a safe haven for the neighborhood kids.

Tell parents that you have Band-Aids for scraped knees, "homework help" for the teen who needs an excuse to avoid peer pressure, time to talk, and a reassuring cookie when something scares a child whose parent won't be home from work for a little while. You might even have a small library of children's books and a soft, comfy chair for curling up in to read. Parents can then tell their children it's okay to knock on your door if they need to.

You are not setting yourself up as a free babysitter or supplanting the parents' role but just extending and nurturing the family, even if you're available only for a few afternoons a week and for emergencies. Your reward will come next Halloween, when your house is not (or is) tee-peed.

The Grouch

What a grouch! He scowls at everyone. There's obviously something wrong with him. Or is there? Have we wished him a good morning or even tried to talk to him? We could approach him in a new way, as though he really is our brother in God's family. "Won't do any good!" you say?

Here's a true story: A woman had been a neighbor of Holy Family Church since it was built. Her family donated much to the parish, including land. But as she swept in front of her home each day, people bypassed her, thinking the bowed head and grim face belonged to an ill-tempered person not worth bothering with. Then some seventh graders from the parish school actually talked with her while distributing flyers. When one said, "We love you," her eyes brightened and her smile radiated. As they left and she turned back to her work, the glow remained with all of them.

The spontaneous act of these kids gave many adults focus—to watch for darkness, light a candle and enjoy the radiance that was there all along.

Click Away Hunger

You're on the Internet anyway, so take a few minutes to do something for the 20 million adults and 13 million children in America who go hungry. Or help save some of the 15 million children worldwide who die each year of hunger.

Go to www.freerice.com and play one of the free educational games. As you work on your vocabulary, geography, foreign language, or other subject, you earn grains of rice which sponsors of the site donate to the U.N. Hunger program. Another time, go to go to www.thebreastcancersite. com, click on the *Hunger* tab on top left, then hit *Click Here to Give—It's Free*. For each click, sponsors of the site donate 1.1 cups of food.

You may find other such websites as you wander around cyberspace. Keep the addresses of all of these sites in an email to yourself, marked "unread," so you remember to go to them often. The breast cancer site is so quick and easy that you can do it each day as you read your email. When you find a similar website, send its address to us and we'll pass it on to others.

A few grains of rice or 1.1 cups of food isn't an awful lot, unless you're one of the people who consider themselves rich if they get to eat something once a day.

TV Commercials

Gotta love those funny TV commercials. How about the ad where one guy hits another in the head with a cell phone twice or where a woman bounces a cue ball off the forehead of an obnoxious man? Then there's the guy who breaks down a wall to be allowed to answer a quiz question. How about those hilarious ones shown during Super Bowl XLI? There were potential suicides (three individuals and one group), self-mutilation, torture, warfare between tribes, people slapping each other, and bank robberies, all of which were designed to be comical.

We're supposed to laugh, of course. If we do, though, what we're telling our children is that violence is both an acceptable response to minor irritants and funny.

It's time to change this way of thinking. We start not by laughing at the aggressive scenes but by using the ads as a chance to talk to our kids about violence against our fellow humans. Our discussion will likely bring out stories of similar antagonism on the playground or among their friends and give us a chance to offer guidance in how to handle such situations. Then again, television violence has been with us since the Three Stooges, and look what a loving world we have.

My Neighbor, My Family

I feel so guilty. I've always swept up my garden debris within an hour after the trash truck has come by and I've taken such pride in keeping my sidewalk clear of all the stuff that blows in from all over. Now, though, my husband's in the hospital and my arthritis is too bad to let me drive to go see him, let alone keep up the house, inside or out.

I've lived here thirty years. People know how neat and clean we are. You'd think a neighbor would notice the mess and come by to check on us.

I'm so alone, but I can't call and impose on them. I'd be a burden. That would make me feel worse. But if somebody just noticed, if they'd just call or drop by, I wouldn't mind. Sure, it would be nice if they'd offer to drive me to see my husband or maybe sweep up out front, but even just a little company would help a lot. I'm just so very lonely and overwhelmed. If only somebody would notice.

Couples TV Dinner

Strengthen your marriage and family by pigging out! Invite a few couples to your home for a potluck TV dinner. Set up TV trays and a buffet dinner, have people load up their plates, then settle in to watch and discuss an informative video. Although the topic may be serious, like communication within families, marriage as a partnership, blending families, or surviving your kids' teen years, the video should be entertaining while fueling discussion. Be sure to stop it at intervals to let people talk about what they've heard. (As host, preview it and take notes on where to stop if there are not built-in discussion-pauses). The informality of the situation encourages your friends to share their stories, and you're likely to have at least as many laughs as serious comments. By the end of this couples-evening you will be full—of good food, good talk, and ideas to enrich your family life.

Videos for Couples TV Dinner

The best type of video for this activity is about relationships and family matters, like handling teenagers. The public library and most church libraries have many of these. Here are some sample titles.

- "Men are from Mars, women are from Venus": Relationship skills. A video found in the public library.

- "Men and Women: Talking Together": Communication skills. A video found in the public library.

- "Real People: On the Journey to Healthy Communication," by Terry Hershey: How to build a relationship and create families from people with different personalities. Available in CD, VCR, DVD, or tape cassette from www. terryhershey.com.

- "Intimacy: Building Healthy Relationships," by Terry Hershey: Defines *intimacy* and explores its risks and rewards. Available from www.terryhershey.com.

- "The Golden Rules: Secrets of Marriage from Couples Married 50 Years or More." Couples discuss their own relationships and how to apply the Golden Rules of Marriage in order to enjoy the romance and fulfillment that comes from a long, happy marriage. A DVD available through online booksellers.

❧ Chapter Six
We Recognize God's Family Throughout the World

"For I was hungry and you gave me food, I was thirsty and you gave me drink, a stranger and you welcomed me, naked and you clothed me, ill and you cared for me, in prison and you visited me....Whatever you did for one of these least brothers of mine, you did for me" (Matthew 25:35-40).

First, Think About It

"It's a small world, after all..." says the song. When we think about it, each of us is connected to millions of others. We talk to Tech Support for a local company, but the person we talk to lives thousands of miles away. We wear clothing that was made in other states and countries. We eat food grown by people in developing nations. We pray at church with people from far away who tell us about their relatives in those places. The largest unifying factor is that every single one of us has the same desire deep in our hearts: peace.

If we're all part of the human family we should act like loving siblings. We should want for them what we want for ourselves, a peaceful and just world.

Such a world begins, believe it or not, in our minds, not in our hearts. If our minds are corroded, the electrical impulses of love can't jumpstart our hearts. That's why so many of the suggestions in this chapter point toward examining our ways of thinking, making changes where they would do some good. Some won't be easy, but all will embrace this ever-shrinking world of ours.

Other Cultures

The idea that each and every person in the world belongs to God seems overwhelming, but it becomes easier as we start to get to know other cultures. One way to do that is an activity that fits in with how we spend our time anyway. Go ahead and watch television, surf the net, browse through the library, help the kids with homework. Before starting, though, choose a third-world or impoverished area you know little about (maybe Africa or Appalachia) and plan to learn all you can about its history and its people, including the hardships they face. Compare your own beliefs and values with theirs. Make a habit of watching for newspaper articles and TV programs about that area and listening for news stories about it. But don't be surprised when you start feeling a kinship with those previously unfamiliar people. That's the idea. That's recognizing just how large your family actually is.

Mix It Up

Look at what she's wearing! I've said this to myself at church, impressed by colorful ethnic dress. However, because I haven't gone up to the person to speak to her, I've missed a chance to get to know someone new and probably learn something about a culture I'm not familiar with.

Too often we miss such chances. People from ethnic backgrounds different from our own are all around us. We can grab the opportunity by sitting with them at church or asking to join their table at fellowship afterwards. We can engage them in conversation at a party, during work breaks, or before and after meetings.

Where and why we are gathered gives us subjects to talk about, like the topic of the meeting or a critique of the day's sermon. Our kids have been doing this since 2002 nationally and locally at Mix It Up at Lunch Day.

If we follow their lead we'll enrich each other's lives and build a stronger human community.

Vacation Time

This was a real fun vacation! I didn't wanna go 'cuz Mom said we'd be in the car a lot. I was mad 'til we got to the first place. There was a lady dressed in pretty cloth and a matching thingy on her head. She showed me how to make a basket and showed me pictures of kids in another place running around playing just like me. Except the kids were black. Then we went to a funny church that had a statue of a fat guy sitting on the altar. A kid showed me how they pray. He was neat, even if his eyes were crooked. We even saw a grocery store that had chickens hanging down from the ceiling. The store–guy laughed when I asked if his 'frigerator was broke. He showed me some icky looking stuff and told me how they still cook it just like they did a hunnerd years ago in some old country.

Then we had tacos for lunch. They were better than Mom's. The cook kept saying something I couldn't unnerstand 'cuz it was another language. Turned out she was saying I could play with her baby. Funny thing was, the baby cried in English. We went to a moo-zeum that had arrows and feathered stuff and pointy tents. Some kids dressed in dead animals danced around and let us join in.

Yeah, I had a lotta fun. I met so many new friends, but I don't know if I'll ever get to see them again 'cuz they live far away. Maybe when I grow up I can find them and we'll have a lot more fun together.

Speak English!

Speak English, darn it. Our blood boils as we wait to be seated at a restaurant, hearing two people near us talking in another language. They're in America, so they should speak English!

But why? Do we think they're talking about *us*? Or planning to rob the place? Do we really *want* (or need) to know what they're saying? If they were speaking in English, it would be rude of us to eavesdrop. We're not bothered by people speaking in sign language or teens speaking their brand of English (although we could do without some of those words).

Most people pepper our everyday language with borrowings from Spanish, German, Yiddish, Italian. Besides, we know that if we go to England, people there will complain that we don't really speak English at all!

Next time, then, resolve to turn boiling blood into thankfulness for living in a country made up of a rich tapestry of cultures, all of which add words to that ever-evolving banquet of language we call "English."

Pen Pals

Remember as a child exchanging letters with a pen pal in another state? How fascinating it was to learn what teenagers in far-away Texas did for fun, or how Joey got to play in the snow for several months in. . . where was that now? You enjoyed being able to experience someone else's life through letters.

Thanks to email (or snail-mail if you prefer), you can do the same thing today on a larger scale. Find out what life is like in Albania or Argentina, Croatia or Costa Rica, Ghana, Rwanda, Uganda, or Viet Nam. In return, tell about your own life. Relearn the fun of having a pen-pal.

Find names by asking people at work or church who have relatives in other parts of the world. Do a search, starting with www.mylanguageexchange. com (international pen pals practicing a foreign language) and www. ppi.searchy.net (Penpal International). Just be sure to avoid singles sites and ones with pictures of women who hope to become foreign brides. After you and your pen pal have communicated awhile, you'll develop a friendship, discovering mutual interests that prove that ours is, indeed, a tiny, interconnected world.

Immigrant Party

Have an Immigrant Party and invite your immigrant friends. Don't have any? Sure you do. All of our kinfolk came from *somewhere* other than the United States. Ask your guests (see sample invitation) to come ready to share their family history—why they came to the U.S., where they landed, what type of community they lived in here, the support system they had (church, neighbors from the same part of the world), languages spoken at home, hardships they encountered here, what they went through to gain citizenship, funny family stories passed down the generations. Maybe each guest could bring pictures of people, places, and documents, as well as a family keepsake that reminds them of those times. You might even want to ask people to bring food to share from one of the cultures each guest represents. Spend the evening sharing your food and your stories.

By the end of the night it will be very clear why you are all friends, because God gave us the oceans not as an obstacle to divide us but as a path to bring us together.

YOU ARE INVITED to an immigrant party

Date_____   Time _____

ADDRESS_____

Given By __Frank & Jackie O'Donnell_ **From** _Ireland & Scotland_

A *what* party? A party only for our immigrant friends. Like you. Even if you are 2ⁿᵈ or 3ʳᵈ generation Americans, you wouldn't be here if it weren't for some immigrants in your family. Look through your family tree and your family mementos and gather up those sad and funny stories you've heard all your life. Then join us for an evening of fun and food.

WHAT TO BRING

- *Stories about where your family came from,* **where they landed, what type of community they lived in here, what kind of support system they had (church, neighbors from the same part of the world), what language they spoke at home and encouraged their children to speak, what hardships they encountered here, what they went through to gain citizenship, any funny or interesting stories you heard growing up.**

- *Old pictures of people, places, events, documents.*

- *Family keepsakes, heirlooms, mementos of your family's early times in America.*

- *A dish to share that might be a family recipe from the Old Country.*

R.S.V.P. by ____[date]____ to tell us you will be coming and whether you will be bringing a main dish, side, salad, or dessert. Call us at 555-5555, or email us at urockem@snodgrass.net.

Be A Refuge

The United States has always been a refuge for those who are persecuted and in danger of losing their lives in their own country. Our hearts open up to displaced families. We recognize the pain of the ostracized widow. We want to protect the orphaned child. We offer sanctuary to the enslaved escaping their bondage. Whenever possible, we try to help refugees who have nowhere else to turn.

What happens to these people once they get here? Agencies do their best to feed and house them until they can settle in and find work. Churches and outreach programs do what they can. What can you do?

If you have room in your home, this is a wonderful opportunity to help someone while giving you and your family the experience of learning about another culture. By offering a refugee a temporary home, you also offer her the human closeness she lost when she left her life behind her. This is especially important to the young people coming to us from war-ravaged countries. In exchange, your guest can introduce you to her own rich culture and heritage, thus helping you destroy stereotypes you didn't even know you had. You might even pick up a new, delectable recipe you wouldn't have thought to try. When you think about it, though, what you're really creating is a recipe for love.

Fair Fundraising

There's a knock at the door. It's a youngster with chocolate bars. You buy because you want to support the soccer team. Warning: in your eagerness to help one group, you may be harming another. Do you know where the cocoa beans came from? Were the growers paid fairly for their work? Enough to feed their families and meet their basic needs? Most likely, the workers, including very young children, are living in poverty in another country and their hard work doesn't earn them enough to climb out of hardship. Meanwhile, fundraisers enjoy big profits, passing on a tiny amount to your soccer team.

Next time your group wants to raise money, suggest a compassionate alternative, Fair Trade Chocolate. For example, there is Divine Fair Trade Chocolate, the first brand in the world to be farmer-owned (www. divinechocolate.com). Or try one of these which are fair to the growers and kind to the earth: www.equalexchange.com, www.Chocolates. com, www.ChocolateBar.com, www.sweetearthchocolates.com, www. DagoboaChocolate.com, or www.VosgesChocolate.com. Some offer discounts for fundraisers. What a deal! The kids raise money, social consciousness, and quality of life for families all at the same time!

❦ *Chapter Seven*
We Reflect God's Image

"...Is not life more than food and the body more than clothing? ...Are you not more important than the birds in the sky?" (Matthew 6:25-26)

First, Think About It

What makes a person a human being is much more than our species or physiology. We were made in God's image, which gives us a kind of nobility. The world we live in, however, seems intent on taking that away from many of us.

As we look around we see people considered not worth interacting with, not valuable enough to protect, good only to hold up to ridicule. They come in all colors, physical conditions, and walks of life. We engage in activities that destroy their human dignity, thus destroying our own. Sometimes we destroy human life itself. Usually we don't realize we're a party to these actions. It's just something we do without thinking.

The following activities call attention to destructive forces that threaten life or quality of life. They'll help remind us that part of being human is exercising our spiritual muscle, our soul.

Jackie O'Donnell

Dumb Blonde

Hear the one about the dumb blonde?

Is there a nationality, ethnic group, age group, or other category of people that you casually make jokes about? Maybe you feel they can't be trusted, that they will cheat or deceive you, or that they're generally not too bright. Maybe you find yourself crossing to the other side of the street at night so you won't come in close contact with them. Just in case.

Examine your innermost thoughts and everyday behavior toward a specific group. Write down ten ways in which "those people" are *similar* to you. Then list examples of actual incidents in which one of "them" cheated, harmed, or scared you or when you had to struggle to make them understand something simple. Think about what was done and said on *both* sides.

Now, mentally stand aside and evaluate. Was there a misunderstanding? Was it only a conflict between people of two distinctly different personalities? Did either of you have preconceived notions that influenced the situation? Was one or both of you impatient or not listening well? Have you ever had a similar experience with someone of a different grouping or even your own?

Such self-examination isn't comfortable for us but is necessary if we are to grow in Him. It gives us an additional reward, as well: a rainbow of new friends to brighten our lives.

Elder Dignity

Some older people experience a loss of self-worth. They no longer have the jobs that made them feel productive or the stamina that made them self-sufficient. People used to value their opinions but now just barely listen to them. How can we help restore their human dignity?

Stop for a chat with the man you often see sitting alone in his front yard as you walk to the grocery store. Call Rita at her senior-living apartment every couple of weeks to exchange news of each other's lives. When Uncle Eddie tells stories about his experience in Vietnam listen attentively, understanding that it has taken him many painful years to be able to talk about it. When tackling a plumbing problem, actually listen to advice given by that neighbor who was a plumber for forty years. Treat these people as you would a valued friend or colleague. Be open and delight in the surprising gifts you receive in return.

More on How To Treat Older Persons

Unlike some other cultures, American society does not honor our elders. There are so many little things that we can do to counteract this trend. Here are a few to get you thinking about what you can do in your own surroundings so that others may maintain their dignity.

1. While walking the dog or walking for exercise, you see a man who spends a lot of time sitting alone in a chair on his front lawn. Stop awhile. Comment on his garden, the weather, how busy the traffic is on the street, or anything else that will help start a conversation. You'll be able to tell by his response if he wants to talk. If so, chat for five minutes before moving on. Each time you pass his way give him a wave and a hello if you don't have time to stop. Better still, allow an extra five minutes for your walk so you do have time.

2. People who used to pride themselves on a tidy yard or house are frustrated that they can't do everything they used to do. It diminishes them in their own minds. They wouldn't feel any better if you made them into your own personal charity. On the other hand, they would appreciate an occasional lawn-mowing offer when you're doing your own or helping each other sort through items that you would then combine and take to a donation center or asking if they had anything to add to the load of junk you were taking to the dump.

3. When it's your turn to make cookies for your daughter's kindergarten class, ask Grandma to help. She can provide labor, maybe a new recipe or short-cut, and some quality conversation.

4. Treat a frail or ill older person with loving respect. Don't just

assume that Grandpa Max needs help getting up off of the couch. Instead, wait to see if he asks for help. If you see him struggling, casually ask if he wants help. If he says yes, go to him and offer him an arm to take rather than reaching and pulling him up.

5. You may think you don't have much to say to Great Aunt Sarah, that you'd just keep repeating the same generalities if you called her often. Not true. Keep a notepad by your phone. From time to time, jot down cute things the kids did, the name of a play or movie you saw, a funny thing that happened at the gas station, a maddening thing that happened in a parking lot, the latest silliness with the new puppy. While talking to Aunt Sarah, note the names of friends or activities she brings up so you can ask her about them in the future. Soon you'll find that you've simply been listening to each other and you won't need your notepad any more.

6. Visit someone at a nursing home. Bring books, family pictures, crafts, CDs and player, or anything else you can experience together and talk about. If possible, get the person out of his room into the fresh air and sunshine. Once you know dietary restrictions, bring in a special treat or plan a picnic lunch for the two of you. Let the person know in advance when you will be coming for the visit so he can enjoy the anticipation as well as the visit. If you don't have a friend or relative in such a facility and are comfortable in doing so, ask at your church if there is someone who could use a new friend.

7. If you're dining out with older people, don't treat them like children who can't understand a menu or who need to be reminded what they should or should not eat. Don't tuck napkins under their chins or onto their laps without being asked. If they say they don't want to take a doggie bag, don't embarrass them with comments like, "But it would make such a nice little lunch for you, Mom." And throughout the meal be sure they're included in the conversation. (If you believe these things don't happen, look around at other tables when you're out.)

8. Stand up for the older person's right to be spoken to directly. Sometimes a server in a restaurant will ask you what your mom wants to order, a store clerk will respond to your dad's question by speaking to you, a doctor will talk to others in the room (to nurses, you, other visitors) as though the patient, because he or she is older, can't hear or understand. Don't tolerate this. Say something like, "Please talk to my dad about that, because he knows better than I do."

Executions

"An eye for an eye." God gave this rule to His people wandering the desert to help them put things into perspective. He knew they often acted out of impulsive vengeance and He wanted them to think before they acted. When Jesus came He refined the Law by emphasizing compassion. Several times a year our society turns its back on Jesus' teaching by executing someone. For example, California seems determined to keep executing men until all 700 men currently on Death Row have been put to death. And Texas executions are frequently in the news.

As followers of Jesus, we must act. We can write letters, send emails, and make phone calls to our governors and state representatives.* They need to be reminded that all life is sacred, even if it belongs to someone who did something terribly wrong. They need to be told again that most Americans favor alternatives like life-imprisonment over execution. Politicians recognize that each stated opinion represents a multitude of silent others who feel the same way. This means that your one little letter DOES have an impact! They know they must listen to us because, after all, elections are coming soon.

*See Chapter 2 for instructions on how to write an effective letter to a legislator.

Movies

DID YOU SEE THAT? The Good Guy is a murderer, the Heroine can't live without sex until the next commercial, and we're expected to cheer at the explosions and applaud the torture of the Bad Guys.

Such is typical television and movie fare. Violence, cruelty, and lust not only sell, they also demean life. This works in total opposition to the attitude of our being made in the dignity of God's image.

Our refusing to watch these programs and movies is a personal step toward following the "We-Attitudes." Moving another step forward, we can explain to our children why our family doesn't watch them, thus raising a more caring, sensitive next-generation. One more step is to write letters to the theater, television station, filmmaker, and advertisers, reminding them that their profits depend on giving us what we want to see. If I do that and so do you and so do our friends and their friends. . . . It's the snowball-effect, possible even in your sunny city.

POD People

People with Obvious Disabilities, or *POD People*, as some of us call ourselves, are often either ignored or "helped" into a worse situation, causing a humiliating loss of dignity. You can help that person struggling on crutches, but ask first. If the answer is "Yes," be supportive of both the person's physical needs and his self-esteem. Here are some ways to do that.

1. If a non-sighted woman needs guiding, let *her* take *your* arm.

2. Someone who has fallen or is having trouble pushing up a hill or curb in a wheelchair is in even greater danger if you just grab hold without asking him what he needs you to do.

3. The disabled woman in the bathroom has only one, single stall she can use, so invite her to go ahead as soon as it's open, and don't use that stall for changing clothes or potty-training your three little ones.

4. Avoid parking in the handicap space "for just a minute" to return a video, and stay out of that cross-hatch zone next to it so the wheelchair ramps on vans can be used without

endangering your car or motorcycle or the person using
his van's ramp.

There are times, of course, when you wouldn't ask a POD if he needs assistance. Instead, you'd just give it by doing nothing. That is, you'd allow the stutterer to finish his own word or sentence and you'd face a lip-reader and speak without exaggerating your lip movements.

Deciding what to do is actually easy. When in doubt, just treat people as you'd want them to treat you.

Ethnic Slurs

Ever hear an ethnic or racial slur and find yourself cringing? That's your conscience responding. At that moment, you are inwardly aware that someone's God-like dignity is being attacked. Deep inside we know that such putdowns only feed bad feelings or stereotypes, keeping them alive, and that they're hurtful rather than healing.

We need to stop tolerating those insults. There are two rules in doing this. First, use a response that is natural and comfortable for you, and, second, make your point but don't humiliate the person you're speaking to. For example, you might say, "That joke makes you sound prejudiced, and I know that can't be true." Or, "My brother-in-law is Irish and he's not a drunk." Sometimes people don't listen to themselves and need someone to draw their attention to what they are actually saying.

More Responses to Ethnic Jokes and Slurs

When you hear an expression that's offensive to a specific ethnic or racial group, let the speaker know it's hurtful. Your comment should depend on the speaker, the situation, and you. Choose a response that is comfortable for you. It should make clear how you feel but flow naturally from your personality. That way, you'll make your point but not come across as self-righteous. You want people to stop and think about what they're saying, but you don't want to embarrass them. Following are some suggestions.

1. If you hear the start of joke at the expense of a group, say,

"Please don't go on. I'm offended by racial (or ethnic) jokes."

2. *At the end of a joke, stare blankly at the teller and say,*

- "Go on. Finish. I'm waiting for the punch line."

- "When does the funny part come?"

- "I don't get it. Why would the person do that in the first place? What makes him so dumb?"

- "I've heard that one before and I still can't figure out what's so funny. How about coming with me so you can tell it to Pastor Hao (or Rabbi Schwartz or my black neighbor, the engineer) so he can explain it to me."

- "You know, my cousin's husband is Scottish and he's one of the most generous people I know."

- "My brother-in-law is Mexican-American, and he's the most energetic, active person I know."

- "Heavens! That sounds like something the KKK would say!"

- "That joke makes you sound prejudiced against Arab-Americans and I know you're not a closed-minded person."

- "Would you believe that I used to think jokes about Koreans were funny? Then I saw how hurt my friend Kim gets when she hears one."

Hey, Dearie
"Hello, Dear."

"Let me do that for you, Sweetheart."

"You want anything else, Honey?"

Guess what, Dearie! I'm NOT your Dear or your Honey or your Sweetheart. You don't even know me. Only my loved ones are allowed to call me by those names.

Why do you do that? I'm an adult. Do you think my wrinkled face makes me feeble-minded? Or do you think that because I move slowly, I need you to be my nursemaid? You know, it could be that I'm quiet because I've learned to talk only when I have something to say. It doesn't mean I can't talk. Or hear, for that matter. So why do you insist on shouting at me?

I think I've lived long enough and been through enough to have earned some respect. How about it?

Jury Summons? Yes!

How can I get out of it? That's our first reaction when we open the notice to appear for jury duty. After all we argue, Jesus said, "Judge not, lest you be judged." However, He was talking not about avoiding making judgments but about judging *righteously.* That means that we shouldn't let those who resent being there or have nothing better to do pass judgment on someone accused of a crime.

God gave us intelligence and compassion, which He expects us to use to fight inequality, manipulation, discrimination, and exploitation—all of which often appear in trials. It takes only one individual, with guidance from the Holy Spirit, to lead the rest of the jurors to the truth of "guilty" or "not guilty."

If you aren't there, who will stand up for justice and human dignity?

Strange People

Who is that strange person? The smiley one who moves and talks slowly while cleaning the tables at the hotdog place. That scruffy-looking guy in the army fatigues asking for donations for veterans outside the grocery store. That strange old man sitting in Starbuck's who keeps trying to talk to me when I'm in a hurry to get my morning coffee. The pregnant girl with all that black makeup—can she even be 15? Who are all those weirdoes around me?

The answer is that they are *people*. Each is a human person with a story, a life; therefore, each deserves dignity.

Try having an actual conversation with them. You may be surprised at how interesting they are. Out in public like that, you're certainly in no danger. The only risk you're taking is learning that these people who seem weird can also be wonderful. In the process, you will have given them the dignity of being recognized as real people.

Sticks and Stones

Sticks and stones may break my bones but words can never hurt me. It was a silly childhood chant. When we grow up, we stop calling people names. Or do we? Hurtful names that have crept into our everyday language are so common that nobody notices, except those people who are affected.

Call me over-sensitive, but as someone who has a physical disability, I'm offended when I hear a stupid act referred to as "lame." My friend has a similar reaction when that same act is called "gay." And the person doing the act? He's "just so retarded." An unexplainable or seemingly strange action is "schtzy," "psycho" or "manic depressive." We talk about the poor as "underprivileged" or "them," somehow different from—and not as good as—us, and we call others "illegals," stripping them of flesh and blood.

We can think before we speak. By doing so, we can shred the sticks and crumble the stones before they have a chance to bruise us.

Chapter Eight
We Protect the Earthly Home God Gave Us

"Learn a lesson from the fig tree. When its branch becomes tender and sprouts leaves, you know that summer is near" (Mark 13:28).

First, Think About It

I know, I know. You recycle every week. You turn off lights when you leave a room and try not to waste water. That's great. However, what we need to do to help our physical world is all of that *plus* start thinking outside the planter box.

What follows are everyday actions we can do that take almost no time but can generate behavior changes and even some family fun.

Our faith demands that we protect our planet and all life on it. So let's get started. In truth, today is the first day of the rest of our Earth's life.

Responsible Drinking

Be a good Christian by drinking responsibly every day. You go to Fellowship, Bible study, meetings, coffee breaks, PTA functions, and soccer matches, accompanied by the ever-present cup of coffee or bottle of water. You stop at Starbucks or 7-11 for coffee. You jog with a bottle of water. So take better care of God's creation by lessening the amount of Styrofoam and plastic on the roadsides and in the landfill. That means actually *using* less of these materials, which really isn't that hard to do.

Keep a coffee cup at your desk and a commuter mug in your car for use at fellowship. Refill a plastic water bottle on your way out to a game. Keep a couple of filled bottles in the refrigerator or freezer (great for a hot day at an arts festival). Just be sure to rotate your cups and bottles often, bringing them home for a thorough cleaning to avoid bacteria growth. Soon you'll learn what the Earth has always known, that those containers last a very long time.

Waste Not

"Consumption has become a habit, a hobby and a sport" (Evy McDonald, *Spending Money as if Life Really Mattered*). Ouch. The truth hurts. I recycle but don't buy items with the chasing arrows symbol/recycled content label. I should prepare more of my own meals, which are cheaper, healthier, and less wasteful. Then there are all those gadgets in my kitchen. Which ones do I actually use and which really make life easier? I can go through my home and give away stuff that's no longer useful or that I'm keeping out of compulsion or the status I think it gives me. I can use the library rather than accumulating books, even visit museums and exhibits instead of buying more dust-collectors.

As an experiment, I plan to set aside a time in which I try not to waste a single thing all day. Then I'll protect two of God's creations at once, the Earth and me. I'll even keep the Sabbath commandment to *rest*!

Grow an Environmentalist

Because today's children seldom get out of the city, not many grow up to choose environmental careers, which results in fewer people to care for our earthly home. You can help reverse the trend and have family fun doing it.

Try shopping together for unusual, Earth-friendly items. Your children will be fascinated by what is available. There are hand-carved bowls made from discarded root balls of Chinese fir trees, decorative stars the Amish make from the tin of old barns, doormats made from the rubber left over in factories that make rubber sandals, unusual herb gardens for window sills, and kits to grow exotic organic mushrooms.

You might even plant a garden with your children. Watch it grow. Enjoy the colors, fragrances, and textures. If you grow vegetables, cook them together to enjoy at a family meal. Or take the family on walks. Your city probably boasts of several beautiful easy-walk trails where you can share nature's sounds, sights, and smells. There are probably parks nearby, too, for picnics or just experiencing the wonders around you. While there, pick up trash and explain to the children that, even if we didn't cause the mess, we should show respect to God by taking care of His gifts. That night your children should be tired enough to sleep soundly, dreaming happy dreams of butterflies and forests.

Garden Care

Spring! Time to reclaim your winter-traumatized yards. This year, try to be gentler with your yard. Would you like vigorous plants without chemicals? How about preventing erosion by wind and water? Or using less water while decreasing the chance of plant-disease?

The answer to all these problems is composting. *But I hate worms*! You don't need the squiggly creatures, or even a container. Start small, with a **compost trench**. Rake those leaves into trenches you've dug between flower beds and then forget them. They'll turn into mulch you can spread around plants or mix into their soil. **Compost pockets** are easy, too. They're 18" deep holes into which you place scraps, like fruit, vegetables, and coffee grinds, and then fill with dirt. In a month, plant something there and watch it thrive.

Compost Awareness Week comes in May, so watch for all the information made available then. That's the time of year for Earth-Day events too, which always have booths promoting composting. Another source for information is the recycling company which services your city. Don't forget the public library, either.

Consider this: by composting, most communities could reuse 50% of the waste they produce. Give it a try.

Animal Experimentation

They're just dumb animals, we're told. But should they suffer needlessly? Some researchers have abandoned what they deem cruel product-testing on animals, explaining that results are questionable (human and animal allergic reactions differ) and can be obtained in other ways (e.g., artificial skin in a test tube). The USDA tries to ensure proper food and shelter for these animals but can do nothing about the infliction of pain or relieving it. Laws are being passed to stop the sale of family pets for clinical trials and to prohibit animal testing when other methods are available. Meanwhile, companies use animals, for instance, to see what eye and skin damage a product causes.

To show your disapproval, boycott their products. Look for a Cruelty Free label on packaging. Go to www.navs.org, click on "Who Tests on Animals," and type in a product or brand. On that same website, order a copy of *Personal Care for People Who Care* to refer to when shopping. Let those companies know that we won't tolerate violence against any part of God's creation.

Fair Game

What a fun day! I didn't want to go to a stupid old Earth Day Fair. Then Dad told me the game we'd play. I'd pick something there and bring it home to do. So could Shari and Mom and Dad.

Shari's project is dumb. She keeps turning off the light when I'm on the pot too long. I thought the black hose Dad and I set up to heat our pool was really stupi, too, but it works. Mom put out a birdhouse and feeder but had to move them over 'cuz of the bird poop. I didn't know we had that many birds in our neighborhood! My Earth Day thing's best of all. I put a bunch of worms in a barrel in our backyard and watch them turn stuff into dirt.

What's really fun is the family rule, that all of us have to help all the others with their project. That means I get to chase Shari around with a bunch of worms and not get into too much trouble. You oughta try this game. It's fun!

Earthly Considerations

Is global warming a lie? Common sense says that the ever-increasing numbers of humans sharing our planet means quicker depletion of its resources, especially if we waste them. Even if I assume that earth's ruin still lies years into the future, doesn't it make sense to try to prevent it or at least put it off even farther?

I can start with small steps. I can't afford a hybrid car but I can avoid Styrofoam, disposable diapers, incandescent bulbs, and toxic garden chemicals. I can adjust my thermostat to more efficient levels and do a better job at recycling, especially flashlight batteries and engine oil. I can air-dry at least some of my laundry. Why, I could go vegetarian once a week! I could even go to Appendix A4 in this book and get more ideas from "What You Can do to Help the Environment." Most importantly, I can start right now to make sure my earthly home stays healthy for my grandchildren.

The Ocean

The ocean gives us beauty, fun, food, jobs, medicine, air, weather patterns, a place to think. In return, we give it pollution, beach erosion, and death to its inhabitants. On the other hand, our normal daily activities can help reverse this destruction. We can lessen pollution by conserving water and guarding against our oil and antifreeze running into the ocean. (Note: the ocean gets more oil from car leaks than from large tanker spills.) We should avoid littering, remembering that cigarette butts tossed onto the street end up washing into the ocean, killing sea-life.

Even choosing our dinner menu helps. Before buying seafood, we can ask questions. Was it farmed, thus depending on wild fish as its food source? Was it farmed inland, meaning that the waste produced didn't flow into the ocean? If wild, was it caught in such a way that didn't also catch turtles, dolphins, and other life that was thoughtlessly discarded?

For help, print and carry a pocket guide from either www.

environmentaldefense.org (click on eco-friendly seafood) or www.
mbayaq.org/cr/crseafoodwatch. If you ever forget and leave your guide
home, take out your cell phone, send a text to 30644 with "FISH" (all in
caps) and the name of the fish and you'll get information on sustainability
on that species.

When we stop to think, we can see how easy it is for us to take better
care of God's wonderful, watery creation.

Let Children Unearth and Old Idea

Children of all ages love to discover things. This is even truer as they
get older. Tell your teenage son for example, that it's important to care
for the earth and he'll tell you how old and uncool you are, but let him
discover it for himself and he'll think his generation invented the idea.

Here's where books come in. For young children, have environment-
related picture and story books available for naptime and bedtime. As they
grow older and are ready for browsing the library, lead them to books
emphasizing Earth-friendly themes. When it's time for a book report,
suggest books that are interesting and easy to read (that will get them),
ones that, incidentally, promote caring for the Earth.

Appendix A5 describes some age-appropriate titles to get your
preschoolers through teens started. The librarian at your child's school or
at the public library can suggest others.

Maybe your children didn't really invent the idea of caring for our
Earth, but they'll become adults who will secure a cleaner, healthier home
for us all.

Chapter Nine
We Accept God's Gift of Peace

"Peace I leave with you; my peace I give to you. Not as the world gives do I give it to you. Do not let your hearts be troubled or afraid" (John 14:27).

First, Think About It

Before you do anything else, examine the meaning you give to the word *peace*. If you think of it as being basically the absence of war, expand your viewpoint. Consider it in these terms: Peace is the absence of injustice, which dehumanizes us all, and the presence of compassion. It's remembering that everyone everywhere is part of the same family and that we're responsible for looking out for our brothers and sisters. It's working each day to build up trust between us, as individuals and as nations. It's cooperation and helping people to help themselves rather than one trying to control another. It means all of us pursuing the common good, being willing to yield to reasonable compromise.

To get to universal peace we must start with ourselves. Someone who is not at peace with himself and his neighbor can't go out and promote peace among others, let alone among nations. Conversely, someone who receives the peace of Christ, internalizes it, and shares it freely will grow butterfly wings that flutter, carrying in its breeze the potential of peace on earth.

Actually, all of the suggestions in this book are aimed at righting or avoiding conditions which interfere with peace. Neveretheless, the following ones ask you to focus your attention on the topic. Be mindful that Jesus gave us the gift of peace not to keep to ourselves but to pass on. Shalom!

Sign of Peace

"Peace be with you." When we say this on Sunday to those around us, we're following Jesus' command (Matthew 5:24) to be reconciled with our brother before approaching the altar. He asks us to make peace with people and to mean it.

Let's expand the circle on Sunday, stretching out beyond those right next to us. Maybe we can plan ahead and choose a seat close to people we dislike, find unpleasant, are angry toward, or whose forgiveness we need. At the Sign of Peace, we'll be close enough to reach out to them, bringing about reconciliation within God's family and, therefore, with the Lord Himself.

In fact, let's take this attitude of harmony with us as we exit the church and interact in the rest of the world. Might that be what Jesus had in mind for us, a world in which His people spread peace? If so, it seems like believing in and living out this loving ritual is a good place to start.

Non-Violence

Lent is a great shot in the rump for our weight-control. That's what many of us use it for. We give up sweets and snacks, hoping to reduce our body-weight. This year, let's concentrate on reducing a different kind of weight in our world, the damaging heaviness of violence, shown in unkindness, hostility, cruelty, disrespect, and selfishness.

The Institute for Peace and Justice has developed a Pledge of Nonviolence we can adopt as an individual, family, church, community, or group of any sort. With it, we make several promises: to respect self and others;

to communicate better; to listen; to forgive; to respect nature; to play creatively; and to be courageous. Read through the explanation of each on the following page. Discuss these actions with your family or group. Talk about how you can go about practicing them in your daily lives. Make a promise to yourself and to the others to start living them today.

When people ask that old Christian question, "What did you give up for Lent?" you can answer, "I gave up being a cause of violence in my world."

Steps Toward Non-Violence

Making peace must start within ourselves, in our families, among groups of friends, at work or school, and within our congregations. Each of us must commit ourselves as best we can to become nonviolent, peaceable people. Here are some steps to follow that will lead us toward that goal.

1. **Respect Myself and Others.** I must respect myself, affirm others, and avoid uncaring criticism, hateful words, physical attacks, and self-destructive behavior.

2. **Communicate Better.** I must share my feelings honestly, look for safe ways to express my anger, and work at solving problems peacefully.

3. **Listen.** I must listen carefully to others, especially those who disagree with me, and consider others' feelings and needs rather than insisting on having my own way.

4. **Forgive.** I must apologize and make amends when I have hurt another person, forgive others, and keep from holding grudges.

5. **Respect Nature.** I must treat the environment and all living things, including my pets, with respect and care.

6. **Play Creatively.** I must promote athletic and recreational activities that encourage cooperation and avoid social

activities that make violence look exciting, funny, or acceptable.

7. **Be Courageous.** I must challenge violence in all its forms whenever I encounter it, whether at home, at school, at work, in the congregation, or in the community, and stand with others who are treated unfairly.

[From "Pledge of Nonviolence for Individuals, Families, and Groups," The Institute for Peace and Justice, 475 East Lockwood Ave., St. Louis, MO 63119.]

Chill Out

Life is hectic. Nothing goes right. My blood pressure soars so I yell at the next person I see. And that feeds my anger. There's no way out of this vicious circle.

That was me a few months ago. I've learned that there's a way to avoid that emotional state to begin with. It took a little work but made my life and temperament a lot better.

Someone explained to me the cause of most disturbances in life. Usually, it's a case of chaos leading to discord. That is, the messier our lives are the more conflict we'll feel. The harder we try to deal with that conflict, the messier our lives get. It's a no-win situation. Was I ever feeling that!

I sat down and took a good look at my routine. I was trying to do too much. I expected too much out of myself and others. I'd make a To Do list, only to find at the end of the day that I'd crossed off just one item but did a bunch of other things not on the list. I was trying to be everything to everybody. Most of all, I was depressed because I never seemed to get caught up. All this caused frustration and rage burning my insides.

Now I'm able to put out the fire before it gets started. How? I've learned to simplify. I began by figuring out four ways I could make my life simpler. I gave up one work-related activity so I could have some breathing time. I stopped obsessing about a meaningless chore—who cares if I didn't make my bed today? I'm working on saying "No" to taking on new tasks. Most important to me, I decided that nothing is as valuable as spending time with my children.

Once I had my four ways, I put them into action. I adopted one a week, although one a month would also work. I practiced that simplification until it became part of me. It got easier as I went along because as my life became more simple my frustrations dissolved, leading me away from anger-inducing situations. I and the people around me are happier and, for me, what used to be issues to go to battle over became issues to be discussed and negotiated.

Now, if we could get world leaders to do the same. . . .

A Lesson From History

If you're a left-brainer who functions best when you get the facts, learn about peace by looking at history. Read about the wars that have scarred our souls in modern times, like the World Wars, Korean War, Vietnam, Iraq, Afghanistan, Bosnia, and Ireland. Go back to our Civil War and the Spanish-American War or earlier. As you read about them, identify the causes for each. There will be an official cause—the reason for waging the war to begin with—and other causes. In fact, the farther away from the conflict that we move, the more objective the analysis becomes.

Make a list of those causes. Probably you'll end up just adding tally marks rather than listing new ones. You'll see recurring themes of one ethnic group believing in their own superiority, another group's secure knowledge that they have a right to a certain piece of land, one intent on keeping specific natural resources for themselves, yet another.... Well, you'll see when you make your list. In all cases the causes boil down to one thing: denying the fact that we are all part of the human family.

Once you have this list, watch the news with an informed eye. When you see one of these causes poking its head out of the swamp of international politics, pray hard and write your lawmakers, insisting that they take action before it's too late. Make sure they know that the action you want them to take is not to run into battle but to have our country be the cool head of reason, bringing people together for the common good of all humanity.

Study history; endorse peace.

Celebrate Peace

Next September 21 celebrate the annual U.N. International Day of Peace. This day, which began relatively small in 1982, now has millions of participants from every corner of the globe. Look for Peace Day events advertised in your area, or go online to find one. On a more personal level, light a candle, meditate, and say a prayer for peace. At noon, with family or co-workers, observe a minute of silence. Write to the President and members of both houses of Congress asking them to make war truly the last resort after all negotiation has been exhausted and to work toward the elimination of nuclear weapons world-wide. With your children, release peace balloons, make origami peace doves and display them, or make peace bracelets they can wear to school. You can come up with other ideas. All it takes is to think PEACE.

Practice Peace

Practice Peace. It's more than just a warm, fuzzy slogan on a tee shirt. It's something we should do every day. Start by forgiving all those slights and hurtful actions aimed your way. They may have been unintentional, anyway. Then learn to take a healing breath before you react to something that upsets you. Next, work on creating more loving relationships, whether it's quickly resolving conflicts between your children or searching out areas of agreement with that co-worker you never seem to get along with.

World peace is a wonderful concept, which will be achieved in God's own time. Meanwhile, let's get ready for that time by practicing peace in our daily lives.

Teach Peace to Children

Some of us are old enough to remember the Flower Children of the '60s and '70s. Although Sunshine and Moonbeam weren't totally on track, they did have one thing right, that peace should be spread.

A more peaceful world begins with our children, who will be the caretakers of the future. We can teach them peace in simple ways. Avoid video games, TV programs, and movies that glorify war, violence, torture, and destruction. As parents, we can be an example by working out disagreements with each other without our engaging in a shouting match and certainly without hitting each other. In fact, even hitting or punching each other in jest sends a message to a child that violence is a game. We can find something to do when we or our children get very angry, whether it's listening to soothing music, reading a book, or sitting quietly in a special spot in the garden. Although no single negative action will necessarily create a violent person, replacing any one of them with a positive action heads a child toward a more serene adulthood.

Family First

Family is the most complicated relationship on earth. They're the people we most love, yet the people who irritate us the most. And they're right there at home, handy for us to take out our rotten day on.

Sociologists say that how we treat each other in our family reflects how we treat everyone else. If we're loving and forgiving within our family, we'll likely extend that not only to our friends but into our attitude toward strangers across the country and in other hemispheres. If we're ready to fight within our family, we're eager to get into conflicts and wars elsewhere. You get the idea.

Then, what small thing can you do? Only you will know the answer. Look at your family and decide.

Name of Jesus (Meditation)

Like all gifts, Jesus' gift of peace is useless unless we accept it. We need to practice it, as well. An effective way is the Name of Jesus Prayer. It's a meditation which takes us out of ourselves and puts us into His loving hands. Here's how it works:

Set aside half an hour and find a quiet, comfortable place to sit (do not lie down). Turn off phones and anything else that might distract you. Settle in, close your eyes, and take several deep, slow, cleansing breaths. Clear your mind. Then, silently or aloud, keep repeating the name "Jesus." You are inviting Him into your being, so you want to drive away any extraneous thoughts. Don't feel frustrated or guilty if a stray thought enters your mind. Just banish it and go back to focusing on the name of Jesus. After about 20 minutes (the timing will come naturally after you've done this a few times—don't keep checking your watch), let yourself slowly return to this world. Take a few more deep, slow breaths and open your eyes. Sit quietly for a few minutes and enjoy the peace that surrounds you. Finally, take that peace with you back into your work-a-day life.

Chapter Ten
Multiple 'We-Attitdues'

"I will show you what someone is like who comes to me, listens to my words and acts on them. That one is like a person building a house, who dug deeply and laid the foundation on rock; when the flood came, the river burst against the house but could not shake it because it had been well built" (Luke 47-48).

First, Think About It

Okay. You've looked at the "We-Attitudes," concentrating on each one individually. You're ready for the advanced course. It's time to try to live several of them at once.

Each activity in this section combines two or more "We- Attitudes." Each is designed to help us adopt a way of life that centers on a socially just world. As you go through, you'll be aware of which "We-Attitudes" are involved. At this point, though, it doesn't matter if you can actually identify them; it matters only that you know that what you're doing is walking in the Spirit of God.

Go ahead and give these a try. There won't be a test at the end, just a better world.

Jackie O'Donnell

More Popcorn, Please

You had so much fun at our Couples TV Dinner Night (see chapter 5), give it another try. Only this time it doesn't have to be couples. Gather a group of interested and interesting people at your house for a potluck, finger food, dessert, or wine and cheese. Show a video which you have previewed and prepared a few discussion questions for. It can be on any topic that speaks to the mind and heart about a social justice issue—the poor or vulnerable, workers' rights, immigration, the environment, human exploitation, discrimination, etc. Let the discussion roll!

This may sound like too much seriousness for a social gathering, but you'll be surprised at how energized people get. Bear in mind that you're inviting people who enjoy a rousing discussion. Why not shake up your little piece of the world? It may lead to understanding and action that shakes some sense into our larger world.

Budgets

Tax time makes us focus on our family budget. It's time to make that focus clearer, to see if our spending habits reflect what we *say* we believe. For example, I believe in human dignity, so shouldn't I stop buying at that huge discount chain that was in the news for hiring undocumented immigrants during the day and locking them up at night? I respect how hard local farmers work, so why not buy at farmers' markets and through co-ops, even though I may have to pay a little more? I can save both money and the environment by walking or car-pooling sometimes. I can forego a night out with business associates and spend a family-centered game-night at home.

As a practicing Christian, I need to make my priorities clear. After all, corporations notice how we spend our money. That makes our family budget a potential weapon of mass instruction!

Prayer

Bless that idiot who can't drive, Lord. Let's face it. When someone does us wrong the last thing we think of is praying for that person, even though it should be our first thought.

Prayer is a powerful gift that God's Word instructs us again and again to use freely. It can change the world, especially if we zero in on specific concerns where we want God's help. For instance, think of someone you think cheated you or otherwise did something bad to you, then pray daily for him. Choose a legislator or other leader and pray for her each day. Focus on an important issue, praying daily for God's guidance for the decision-makers. When it's election time, pray that the voters will make sure that the best people and the most just laws win. You might go a step farther and form a small prayer group to meet weekly to pray for an issue.

When you see results—and you will see them within yourself and in those you pray for—remember to thank God for being such a good listener.

Be Aware
"Here I am, Lord...," we often sing, inviting Him to send us where He wants us. Then we don't wait for an answer.

We know it's silly to expect a phone call or letter from Him. But how often do we look around to see if, just maybe, He *has* answered? There's that out-of-work man you keep running into and an opening where you work. There's the ill neighbor and you do go to the grocery store weekly anyway. There's the lonely stranger in the room you pass on your way to visit your dad at the nursing home and you really do have an extra fifteen minutes. You have the ability to speak convincingly and you learn that the City Council will be discussing a harmful resolution the very night you'll be at a meeting elsewhere in the building.

How can God use us if we don't respond to the situations He puts us in? How can *we* respond if we don't open ourselves to recognize His nudges, if we don't allow ourselves to be aware?

Signing Petitions
Don't sign your life away. That's what you may be doing if you take the petition thrust at you and sign it just so you can get your frozen groceries home before they melt. Read that petition before signing it. Don't ask the person with the clipboard for clarification because, if passed, the law will

say what the petition says, not what you or the signature-gatherer hopes it will accomplish. Understand that the gatherers have their own agenda, whether it's to be paid for another signature or to get their viewpoint passed into law.

Look closely at it. Is the wording clear and specific? Do you want the law to be exactly as what's written on the petition? Most importantly, does everything in it conform to the "We-Attitudes"? If so, sign it. Otherwise, walk away.

Signing a petition is a small but important step toward changing unfair, oppressive, discriminatory laws. Let's just make sure we vote in the ethical laws we think we're asking for.

Relaxing Reading

Sunshine, a comfy lawn chair, a cool drink, and a good book. Now, there's a recipe for a nice summer day. If you want to combine relaxation with something worthwhile, read up on a social justice issue. The library is filled with great novels with such themes, as well as biographies of fascinating people like Dorothy Day, Mother Teresa, Cesar Chavez, and Martin Luther King., Jr. Explore a major issue you've been struggling with, like immigration, the death penalty, elder care, hunger, ethics in business, poverty, war, abortion, global climate, violence—yes, all these are issues of social concern. Become more familiar with what Christian social teachings have to say about our responsibilities as Christ's disciples.

To get you started, find the Bibliography in Appendix A6. It lists book titles, with annotations to give you an idea of what each book is about. Choose a title or two and pick up a copy at the library or book store. Then settle into that lawn chair for a quiet read. While you're laid back sippin' and sunnin', you may learn how to simplify your life and save the world at the same time.

Classic Films

It's drizzly weather, but the kids need something to do. Show them a thought-provoking classic movie. Afterwards, talk about what they saw, what went on and why, then relate it to real people in real situations today.

Encourage questions and reactions. "Could some kid I know face going to prison for killing his dad?" (*Twelve Angry Men*). "But poor people *today* can get jobs and not have people disrespect them" (*Grapes of Wrath*). "How dumb! People can't be accused of stuff just because of their color!" (*To Kill a Mockingbird*).

Find many of these films at the public library. Scan the television guides for others. For instance, *Ox Bow Incident* and *Diary of Anne Frank* show up often, as do *Gandhi, Eye on the Prize,* and *Play it Forward.* Check video rental stores for *The Hiding Place* or *Schindler's List.* Your friends who are movie buffs probably have a film they'd recommend and lend you, too. Gather the kids and start the movie.

Hey. How about passing me the bowl of M&Ms?

Wear Your Heart

Summer is tee-shirt weather! It's time to dig out the old ones and buy some new ones. It's also time to think about what slogans or pictures are on those shirts. After all, when we dress we become a walking billboard for what we believe. One set of beliefs is described by these sayings, actually seen on shirts: "It's All About Me;" "Silence is Golden, Duct Tape is Silver;" "Orgy of Hate;" "The last hope for humanity rests on a high-powered machine gun;" "A woman's place is chained to the stove." Then there is the fuzzy-headed kid urinating on a person of a clearly definable ethnic origin.

Other beliefs are expressed, of course, not only by crosses and religious references or Biblical quotes, but also by "I ♥ [person or place]," "World's Greatest Mom," "Do random acts of kindness," and pictures of a grandchild or multi-ethnic group linking arms.

The question to ask ourselves is, "Does what I'm wearing reflect who I am inside?"

Now, about those bumper stickers....

Take Jesus To Work Day

On Take Your Child to Work Day you include your children in your work (and show them off). Why not do the same with Jesus? Each Tuesday, for example, focus in turn, on one of the "We-Attitudes." Today, do something to ensure human dignity, like speaking up when you hear a degrading ethnic joke. Next week, strengthen family by helping someone so he can go home on time for a change and not miss his son's ballgame. The following week, promote the company's United Way drive. Next, go in with a co-worker on a microloan. Week 5, thank those "invisible" support people, like the janitor, cafeteria worker, mailroom clerk, or office go-fer. Week 6, eat lunch with someone from a cultural background different from yours. Week 7, head up a campaign to ban Styrofoam and plastic bottles from your office.

You could do this one day a month instead and you can choose other activities that fit the "We-Attitudes." This book contains many ideas. Because you've invited Jesus to your job with you, He'll be there to help. Together, you'll work toward a more just world.

And if people see the hand of Christ in your actions, that's a bonus.

There Ought To Be A Law

Do you believe you know how to solve a problem related to hunger, poverty, violence, discrimination, or other evils damaging people's lives? We've all said, "I wish they'd..." instead of actually *telling* someone who is in a position to do something.

Californians have had a vehicle in State Senator Joe Simitian's annual There Ought to be a Law contest. During the Fall, people submit proposals for a new law or arguments for deleting an old one. He chooses at least one idea and introduces it as a legislative bill in the Spring. (For details and entry form, go to his website, www.senatorsimitian.com). Winners are treated to lunch at the State Capitol and often asked to testify in behalf of their bill. Even if your idea isn't chosen, you alert a lawmaker to a problem and potential solution, encouraging him to become more involved.

Not a Californian? Tell your state representative that his constituents have some good ideas and you think he should offer them a similar chance to express themselves.

Calling attention to society's ills is an important first step toward making meaningful changes that will help the people who are caught up in those ills.

Chapter Eleven
Special Days
Special Opportunities

Jesus' first miracle took place at a wedding feast, and "so revealed his glory, and his disciples began to believe in him" (John 2:11).

First, Think About It

Time to celebrate. You've made it this far, so why not? We as Christians and as Americans enjoy a multitude of holidays during any given year. We spend them enjoying a day off, firing up the barbeque, having friends over for a get-together, going to church to thank God for His great love.

Here we highlight ten prominent special days, both secular and religious, and invite you to take what you've learned about living a socially just life into those occasions. If we allow it, every one of them will remind us of what God has done for us and what He hopes for in the lives of all of us.

Have a good holiday, one that brings blessings to you and to everyone your spirit touches.

New Years

Two more weeks to make New Year's Resolutions. May as well forget the traditional weight-loss one, since we fail before February anyway. We could resolve to quit smoking or swearing, be more organized or thrifty. Then, again, we could step out from our own little world into the larger one.

Make this the year to help protect and nurture a child. Yes, you can send money to support a child on another continent, but you may wish to make it more personal. One way is to volunteer at a local hospital as a person who cuddles at-risk infants, giving them the warm contact that will save their lives. Another is to become a Foster Grandparent, Big Brother/Sister, or Child Advocate. Also, do something when you see that timid first-grader being bullied by other kids. And spend more time with your own children or grandchildren, playing games, taking walks, and providing times for talk to happen.

Focusing on children is a resolution that makes a brighter year for everybody.

Martin Luther King Day

God has a dream—a world of peace and justice for all His children. He *could* make it happen with a mere thought. However, He gave us free will and a conscience to help us do what is right. He sent us people like Martin Luther King, Jr., to show us that the way to achieve such a world is not through violence but through acts that unite us as God's family.

Most of us aren't as bold as King. Nor do we have to be. Mainly, we require a true desire to see God's dream fulfilled. We start by asking for direction, with a simple prayer like, "Father, today make me aware of an injustice happening around me and tell me what you want me to do about it." Repeat this prayer daily and listen for His response, probably in opportunities that arise seemingly out of nowhere.

A child will be in danger. A dying friend will need companionship. A racial slur will upset you, leading you to challenge the speaker. You'll learn of and join an email campaign to stop an execution. You'll meet two people, one who has a spare room and one who is homeless, and be able to match them up. You'll discover that a favorite store treats its employees unfairly, so you'll stop shopping there and you'll clearly tell them why. A proposition will jump out at you from election materials and you will vote in a way that fosters justice. A jury notice will arrive and you'll gladly serve so that you can help guard against the inequities that often occur in our legal system.

These are answers to our prayer, inviting us to do something specific. Will our act transform the world? Jesus' first sign, changing water into wine at Cana, seemed of little importance, yet it was world-changing, because it "revealed His glory, and His disciples began to believe in Him."

Today, God gives us chances to perform other small miracles to help fulfill His plan. In short, He shares with us His dream of peace on earth and justice for all members of His family. But only if we actually listen to Him.

Easter

Happy Easter! Yes, the actual day was last week. But we are still in the Easter season. If we've left behind the joy of His rising and gotten back to our daily routine, we aren't the Easter People we claim to be. Jesus didn't rise in glory so we would have a single day to celebrate; rather, He rose to change the world, which is exactly what He expects us to do.

We honor Him by taking His peace to others, especially those vulnerable people we've failed to protect and those members of His family we've turned our backs on.

Easter season is the perfect time to recognize injustices and try to rectify them, whether in the workplace, our community, or the world. It's a time to restore human dignity to people who have lost it through no fault of their own. It's time to celebrate life, to work toward stopping the destructive forces of suicide, genocide, executions, poverty, and damage to our environment.

Christ gave us the *Humanity User's Guide* through His teachings. It's up to us to follow that guide now, during Easter season and throughout the year.

Jackie O'Donnell

Mother's Day

I am like Mary. So are you. At least, as people who receive Jesus, we should be. Mary was given a choice whether or not to carry and nurture Jesus. When she said "Yes" she did so with trust in and submission to God's will. Isn't that what we do each time we celebrate Communion? Our act of consuming and our reverent "Amen" show our acceptance of all that God wants for us.

Although the Bible doesn't tell much about Mary, we see her concern for others at the marriage feast and with the Disciples. She even made that long trip to see Elizabeth while in the midst of her own pregnancy. Her life couldn't have been easy, with the town gossips painting her as either crazy or a fallen woman, and she was living during dangerous, turbulent times. But she had yielded so completely to God's will that reaching out to others was natural to her.

We should do no less as we, too, carry Jesus and the Holy Spirit within us. We can show our outrage at the violence we see around us. We can work toward a better life for the poor, the homeless, the immigrant struggling to make a future. We can embrace a frightened child or visit shut-ins to remind them of their dignity and worth. We can tell our law-makers that we won't tolerate laws that harm a group of people or the environment or our reputation as a peace-loving, fair-minded nation.

God doesn't expect any of us to solve every problem. All He asks is that we be like Mary and use the Bread of Life He places within us to feed each other.

Father's Day

Joseph was the ultimate foster-father. His responsibility began with dedicating the baby Jesus according to Mosaic Law and continued with teaching the youngster a trade. Always, he had to be a good example so that Jesus would grow up properly. In other words, Joseph is the model for all men, whether they have their own children or not.

Even a childless man has ample opportunity to grow into the amazing role modeled by Joseph. He can become an unofficial Foster Grandparent or Big Brother to his divorced sister's son, spending time with him so the boy feels positive masculine influence in his life. He can help out with teen activities at church or with other youth groups. He can get the neighborhood bully to help fix up a project-car, thus giving the boy something to do that proves his worth to himself. If a man wants to become more involved, he can join Child Advocates or a similar group and help a young person navigate his home situation and the legal system.

Whatever a man chooses to do, he can make every day into Father's Day!

Independence Day
Happy 4th of July! Watch fireworks displays and get that BBQ going. Play with the kids. Relax with a cold drink. And reflect on what the day celebrates, Independence for all Americans.

Take a moment to think about our countrymen who can't enjoy full independence because of their social, physical, or financial situation. Think about what Jesus would want us to do about them. Then make this commitment to work for social justice:

As a disciple of Jesus I promise to

- *PRAY regularly for greater justice and peace.*

- *LEARN more about Christian social teachings.*

- *REACH across boundaries of religion, race, ethnicity, gender, family life, and disabling conditions.*

- *LIVE justly in my household, school, work, the marketplace, and the political arena.*

- *SERVE those who are poor and vulnerable, sharing more time, talent, and treasure.*

- *GIVE more generously to those in need at home and*

abroad.

• *ADVOCATE for public policies that protect human life, promote human dignity, preserve God's creation, and build peace.*

• *ENCOURAGE others to work for greater charity, justice, and peace.*

Labor Day

"Honor labor" isn't merely a union slogan. It's a concept that's interwoven into God's Word. In the Parables, those who worked received a just wage. The Disciples and Jesus Himself worked, gathering fish and grain and souls.

Today, let us pause and think about all of our fellow-workers who often go unnoticed except by those who would take advantage of them: janitors at a major supermarket chain who are being denied days off, breaks, overtime and a safe work environment; hotel workers whose workload and injuries increase while owners continue to under-staff; people whose employer, a huge discount store, provides little or no health care, forcing them onto public assistance programs; the 59,600 children under age 14 employed illegally last year, many in fields, factories, and sweatshops here in our own country.

Scripture tells us to *"be doers of the word and not hearers only"* (James 1:22). The orphans and widows we are told to care for (James 1:27) refer back to the Old Testament, where they were symbols of everyone who is oppressed. That means that just thinking about exploited workers is not enough. We must do something to help them. We must find ways to get involved, to change their lives for the better. We can be aware of companies that treat their employees unfairly, then boycott them and let them know why we are doing so. We can support the workers, in our prayers and on the picket lines. We can urge our law-makers to action. We must, above all, keep these workers in our hearts. For, as Mark's Gospel (Mark 7:6-8) points out in its quote from Isaiah, it is all too easy to honor God with our lips while our hearts are far from Him.

Honor labor. Honor God.

Election Day

Another darn election! It never comes out the way I'd vote. It's just a waste of time and money.

Actually, it will be a waste if you *don't* vote. Even if there's only one issue you really care about, make your voice heard on it. Better still, take some time to get acquainted with more of the issues on the ballot. They tend to be social justice issues, since they determine how we treat our fellow human beings, including our family, co-workers and the poor, even us voters. Find out about them from www.smartvoter.org (League of Women Voters), www.usccb.org (U.S. Conference of Catholic Bishops), or other websites or organizations.

If you haven't registered to vote, do it NOW. You can even vote from the comfort of your own home by applying for an absentee ballot. Why bother? Because not voting would let a small handful of people make decisions you're forced to live with, decisions that are contrary to Christ's teachings. Think and pray about those people and issues, then VOTE!

Thanksgiving

Today I give thanks for a world that is isn't here yet but can be if we follow the "We-Attitudes." It's a world where *all* human life is respected and we give God's unselfish love to others, thus protecting our families and communities. Everyone's basic human needs are met and we work for the common good. Our business, governmental, and personal policies help people improve their own lives. The nobility of work is recognized and all people have decent work and fair wages and own private property. We believe we *are* our brother's keepers, because we are a human family sharing a world. And we show our respect for God by being good stewards of all His creation.

I thank God for this view of the world and for sending *you* to help build it.

Jackie O'Donnell

Christmas

Start a new Christmas tradition. Each family member takes a slip of paper and writes down his name, along with the gift he's giving and places the paper in a special stocking or wrapped box with a slot on top. The gift should be for someone outside your family, like a neighbor, another family, an acquaintance from church, or a person you've heard about. The gift must be of time, not money or goods, a gift of *self*, not charity.

Here are some examples: monthly visits to a nursing home for a year; driving a person to medical appointments until he's well; helping an adult or child learn English or to read or write; changing the attitude of a prejudiced friend. Look through this book for other ideas.

Christmas morning, as a family, open and read these "gifts" and agree to help each other follow through on them. This is the kind of gift-giving Christ expects of us, that makes a real difference to the people who receive our gifts as well as to our own hearts.

Holy Christmas, blessed year!

❧ *Chapter Twelve*
Where to Now?

*I*n the lines below, copy a short passage or verse in which Jesus spoke to you through Scripture, one you can memorize and carry with you into your life as you follow His teachings and work to make the world a more just place for everyone.

_____

_____

_____

_____

_____

And Keep Thinking About It

Look back at what you've done. Even if you've tried only half of the suggestions in this book, you've shed your cocoon and taken flight as a beautiful butterfly. You, just one, single person, added to other emerging butterflies, are helping to make changes in our world which will grow and spread, leading us closer to what God wants for us.

Jackie O'Donnell

Stretch your wings. Experience more of what you've read in this book. Keeping the "We-Attitudes" in mind, find other small ways to live your life in a compassionate, socially just way.   Flutter your wings just a little bit every day and know you're truly affecting the world.

In fact, let us know about your experiences. Leave a message through one of our websites—www.SmThingsCount.com or www.JackieODonnell. net.

Above all, remember this: small things really *do* count!

❦ *Afterword*

It's only fitting that we end with a quote from the woman who inspired this book, Mother Theresa of Calcutta. By listening to Jesus, she found ways to bring His love into places others prefer to think don't exist. Through her acts of kindness and her no-nonsense words to politicians and the common man, she made the world aware of the plight of God's vulnerable children. The small things that she did changed the lives of so many people. She says:

People are often unreasonable and self-centered.

    FORGIVE THEM ANYWAY.

If you are kind, people may accuse you of ulterior motives.

    BE KIND ANYWAY.

If you are honest, people may cheat you.

    BE HONEST ANYWAY.

If you find happiness, people may be jealous.

Jackie O'Donnell

BE HAPPY ANYWAY.

The good you do today may be forgotten tomorrow.

DO GOOD ANYWAY.

Give the world the best you have, and it may never be good enough.

GIVE YOUR BEST ANYWAY.

For you see, in the end, it is between you and God.

IT NEVER WAS BETWEEN YOU AND THEM ANYWAY.

--Mother Teresa

❦ *Appendix A*

A1. HOW TO SHOP FOR CAUSES

Places to Shop for Causes

Brand name *Red*: A partnership of companies which give proceeds to the Global Fund to Fight AIDS, Tuberculosis, and Malaria. Look for products (all red-themed) from American Express, Converse, GAP, Giorgio Armani, and others.

U2's Bono's *One* campaign against poverty: Tee shirts made in Africa by Edun, a fair-trade label created by Bono and his wife, Ali Hewson. Alos, U2 and Greenday songs put out to support charities.

Items to Support St. Jude Children's Research Hospital: One-of-a-Kind Plush Elephant Gift Card Holder, truffles, Christmas cards—found at Target Stores. Products have an easily-identifiable St. Jude magnifying glass on their labels.

Salvation Army Charities: Angel Christmas ornaments and CDs ("Songs for the Greater Good") featuring various artists.

Christopher Radko Christmas Ornaments: Macy's has donated a portion of the proceeds from these to charities devoted to animal care.

Jackie O'Donnell

Museum of the African Diaspora: Beaded necklaces, bracelets, bags, and pins. Part of sales go to HIV/AIDS-infected orphans in South Africa.

Organic Bouquet: An online florist. Portion of sales of some of their bouquets go to charitable causes like the American Red Cross, PETA, Mercy Corps, CoOp America, and the National Wildlife Federation.

Breast Cancer: The pink ribbon on a label means that some of the proceeds are supposed to go to fight breast cancer, but be careful (see warning below). Various companies also offer special fund-raising sales. For example, in 2007 Riedel Crystal offered its limited-edition Riedel Pink Cinum Rose set, a clear glass bowl and foot with pale pink stem. Fifteen percent of each sale went to Living Beyond Breast Cancer, a non-profit which helps breast-cancer survivors improve their lives. Sales of similar glasses in 2005 and 2006 raised $100,000 for the group.

Clothing and cosmetics: October is the best month to watch for these fund-raising products. Watch the ads in the newspaper and on television.

Be careful

Check the company to see how much is actually going to a cause and what cause it is really going to. For instance, many product labels display the pink ribbon designating the fight for breast cancer, but some companies donate very little or cap their contribution at a specific amount, and some use the ribbon to call attention to breast cancer (especially during October, Breast Cancer Awareness Month) but give nothing toward research or treatment. Go to www.thinkbeforeyoupink.org, the Breast Cancer Action website to check on a product. For all products, try to find out how much money will be donated, including both the company's minimum and maximum and what time period is covered by the donation-campaign.

Make sure the charity is reputable, too. Help can be found at www.give. org (Better Business Bureau Wise Giving Alliance), www.bbb.org (Better Business Bureau), www.komen.org (Susan G. Komen Foundation), www.CharityNavigator.com, or www.ag.ca.gov/charities/faq.htm (for California-based organizations) or your state's equivalent.

What is considered acceptable? A charity should spend 75% or more for programs, a maximum of 15% for administration, and no more than 10% on fundraising.

Phone solicitations: don't give in. Very little of what you give through a phone solicitor actually goes to the charity's programs unless the charity itself is doing the telemarketing rather than a telemarketing company. How do you tell? It's difficult. Asking doesn't guarantee an honest answer.

Donating a vehicle: It's hard to determine how much actually goes to the charity. IRS rules say the charity has to report to the IRS the full value of the vehicle, even though they don't get that amount when selling it. Besides, the charity has expenses related to that donated vehicle, ones they must pay to private companies.

Fundraising costs are sometimes hidden in programs. A case in point is the charity that mails out educational material which has as its main purpose asking for donations.

A2. HOTLINES

Phone 211 (not available yet in all areas): help in various languages with food, shelter, senior services, addictions, counseling, and other needs.

Adolescent Suicide: (800)621-4000

Al-Anon/Alateen: (888)425-2666

Alateen: (800)352-9996

Alcohol/Drug Abuse Hotline: (800)662-4357

Cancer (patients and family): (800)422-6237 or www.cancer.org. Type in your zip code to get to an online community of cancer survivors and families to chat with 24/7.

Child Abuse: (800)342-3720 or (800)422-4453

Cocaine Hotline: (800)992-9239

Compassionate Friends: families following the death of a child (877)969-0010 or www.compassionatefriends.org

Domestic Violence Hotline: (800)829-1122 or (800)548-2722

Domestic Violence/Child Abuse/Sexual Abuse: (800)799-7233 or (800)942-6908 (Spanish Speaking)

Eating Disorders: (888)236-1188

Elder Abuse Hotline: (800)252-8966

Marijuana Anonymous: (800)766-6779

National Domestic Violence Hotline: (800)799-7233

National Drug Information Treatment and Referral Hotline: (800)662-4357

Pregnant and Young Hotline (Birthright): (800)550-4900

RAINN National Rape Crisis Hotline: (800)656-4673

Rape, Abuse and Incest National Network: (800)656-4673

Runaway (Confidential): (800)231-6946

Self-Injury Hotline: (800)366-8288)

Seniors Legal Hotline: (800)222-1753. Free legal assistance for people over 60. At www.seniorlegalhotline.org you can write out a question and an attorney will call you back.

Sexual Abuse: (888)773-8368

Suicide/Depression: (800)784-2433

Youth Crisis Hotline: (800)448-4663 or (800)422-0009

A3. HOW TO WRITE TO PRISONERS

<u>Finding a Prisoner to Write</u>

- Write someone you know or a friend or relative of someone you know.

- Check with people who already write prisoners. Get them to ask the ones they correspond with to recommend someone at their prison who would be interested in receiving mail from you. (This even screens them for you.)

- Go to a website like www.writeaprisoner.com and select a name. (Do an Internet search for other sites).

<u>Before You Write that First Letter</u>

1. *Are you age 18 or older?* If not, don't write. It could get the prisoner into trouble.

2. *Get a post-office box.* Unless the prisoner is someone you already know, it is unwise to give him or her your address, let alone your phone number. Presumably, the person you write to will simply be a good person who made a mistake. You don't know, though, if he might show up on your doorstep later on expecting you to take charge of rebuilding his life. He can't do that if he doesn't know where you live.

3. *Understand that your letters will be opened and read by prison staff.* This shouldn't be a problem for you, because you wouldn't write anything that would cause trouble for the prisoner or that you wouldn't want a stranger to

know.

4. *Make sure you're at ease with this activity.* If you're fearful of people who are serving time, don't write. If you're uncomfortable communicating with strangers, don't write. If you just want to write once or twice then drop it, don't write.

5. *Make sure you can avoid becoming a co-dependent.* As you get to know your inmate-friend, you may very well start feeling sorry for him and want to take him on as a cause. Don't. If you do, you invite being taken advantage of and you do the inmate no favors. After all, your purpose is to give him a link with the outside world, to let him know he can make a new life when he is released; it is not your purpose to adopt and parent him either inside or outside prison.

Your First Letter

1. *Introduce yourself.* Explain how you came to write him, how you became interested in writing prisoners, and how you found his name. If you know anything about what put him behind bars, you might mention that, as well as how you know. Tell a little about yourself: marital status, children, job, hobbies, your personality, something that makes you happy, something that makes you mad. You can mention your religious beliefs, but don't preach. The idea of this letter is to give the recipient a feel for who you are so he can decide whether or not writing you would be a mutually enjoyable experience.

2. *Ask about the mailing rules of the particular prison.* Rules vary, especially concerning what can be sent through the mail. Your new friend will be able to send you a copy of the regulations. Failing to follow them means that your letters will be returned to you or destroyed.

3. *Keep it fairly short.* If you send a dozen pages you may overwhelm the person. All you want to do is let him know a little about yourself and see if there's interest in corresponding.

Every Letter

1. *Always include your name and address (P.O. Box) in the return-address section of the envelope.* This is so your letter can be returned to you if there's a problem. Also, letters that don't show their origin may not get through to your intended recipient.

2. *Don't expect an answer.* If you're writing someone out of the blue, he may never answer. There may be something about your letter that makes the person feel you wouldn't click as correspondents, so he chooses not to respond. If so, don't take it personally. It happens every day when we meet new people. Move on to another person who might respond better to you.

3. *Don't expect a quick answer.* Mail must be examined for contraband and illegal messages, which means mail rooms often get backlogged. Inmates may receive letters within a few days or several weeks or even longer. They can't answer what they haven't received! Moreover, their meager supply of stamps may have temporarily run out.

4. *Be informal and friendly.* Write about activities you and your family like to do. You can even send a few photos (check the mailing regulations first), a drawing your child made, a page of tasteful jokes, or information on a sports team or news event your inmate has shown interest in. Be creative!

5. *Avoid pity-statements and lectures.* They don't need to hear about how brave or ill-treated you think they are, let

alone how poorly life has treated them. And they certainly don't want to be told that it's their own fault that they're incarcerated. If you wouldn't want to hear it, don't say it to them. Later, you may get to know each other well enough that such topics are acceptable, but not at the beginning.

6. *Ask non-threatening questions.* What your new friend writes will give you a clue as to whether he's willing to talk about his case or his family or prison life or whatever. Ask general questions so he has something to write you back about. But don't get too specific or personal, because you are strangers trying to build a communication path.

7. *Be honest.* If you're asked something you don't want to answer, don't make up excuses. Instead of saying things the inmate will see right through, like "It's illegal for me to tell you my address (or phone number)," say that you prefer not to give it out to someone you haven't met personally. He will understand and not be hurt.

8. *Be human.* If you've had a bad week, you don't need to dwell on it in a letter, but you also don't need to avoid it. Although you probably won't want to go into all the gory details, a complaint about your unreasonable boss or your sloppy teenager makes you a real, live human being.

In General

- Try to write often, at least once a month. Yours may be one of the few letters he receives.

- If asked for stamps, you may choose to send some. Postage is expensive when top pay for prison jobs (which very few earn) is 99 cents an hour. But check the prison's mailing regulations for how many you can send at a time.

- Do not send money.

- Enjoy getting to know your new friend and at the same time, helping him feel connected with the outside world in a way that gives him hope that he can make a crime-free life for himself once he's released.

A4. WHAT YOU CAN DO TO HELP THE ENVIRONMENT

1. Take recycling seriously as a family, setting up easy-to-reach containers for items you'll return for cash to a center and for those to be picked up at your curb weekly. Be sure all family members use them.

2. Have a cat? Choose kitty-litter made from corn cobs, wheat, sawdust, wood shavings and chips, peanut shells, recycled newspaper, orange peels, or other natural materials.

3. When taking the family dog on a walk, pick up his "gifts" with biodegradable poop bags. To be even kinder to the environment, bring the bag home and flush the contents.

4. When shopping for toys for pets, bypass the rubber and plastic ones, which are often not earth-friendly, and go to the ones made of recycled materials.

5. Wash clothes in cold water and use low- or phosphate-free detergent. Air-dry laundry whenever possible.

6. Instead of paper towels, use dish towels or cloth to wipe up spills and for cleaning windows and kitchen surfaces. Wash and reuse them.

7. DO use the dishwasher. It uses less water than hand-washing (save 20 gallons a day). But Do NOT pre-rinse dishes, which is not needed with modern machines and wastes 2½ gallons of water per minute. Run full loads, use the lightest setting to do the job, and open the door to let dishes air dry.

8. Need a computer for college? Buy one of the energy-conscious models now available. The fan doesn't blow constantly, and it runs more efficiently.

9. Reduce use of nonessential appliances (e.g., electric can openers and pencil sharpeners). Unplug household appliances when not in use (they still draw energy even when turned off.) Replace them with Energy Star efficient models.

10. Minimize disposables. Use reusable containers for sandwiches and leftovers instead of plastic wrap, baggies, and foil. Use rechargeable batteries. Use cloth diapers, or at least alternate between cloth and disposal. If you must buy disposable products, make them paper or glass.

11. Return reusable items to merchants (e.g., plastic and rubber pots to nursery, hangers to dry cleaner).

12. Buy safe but used sports equipment from thrift stores and sports shops specializing in used equipment.

13. Buy products that will last; rent items you will use only once or twice, then store for years before tossing them into the landfill.

14. Do home maintenance. Fix leaky pipes, tune up your furnace, insulate and weather-strip your house, keep dryer, furnace ,and air filters clean.

15. Insulate your water heater and set it at 130 degrees, which is cool enough to save energy, but hot enough to kill bacteria.

16. Conserve water inside your home. Install low-flow aerators on faucets and water-saving showerheads. Do not leave water running when showering, shaving, brushing your

teeth, or washing dishes. Place space-occupiers in toilet tanks. (Do not use bricks or rocks, as they can damage pipes.)

17. Conserve water in your lawn and garden. Water before 7AM (saves 15-40 gallons of water per day) and only three days a week (all that most gardens need). Use soaker hoses, drip irrigation, or a sprinkler that spreads large drops of water (mists waste water through evaporation). Collect rainwater and gray water from tub, sink, or laundry for use in gardening. Landscape your home with rocks, wood chips, or native plants, which use little water.

18. Lessen energy use in your home. Lower thermostat one degree for every hour you will be away or asleep. Turn off lights when you leave the room. Replace incandescent bulbs with energy-efficient bulbs. Use draft-stoppers to block the cracks between exterior doors and floors

19. Watch what you eat. Buy fresh. Buy organic produce (no chemicals to pollute the earth). Buy locally produced items from farmers' markets if possible (long-range trucking adds to pollution). Eat a vegetarian diet one day a week (the meat industry is one of our heaviest polluters).

20. Learn about the dangers of everyday household products and use alternatives instead. For example, avoid dish soaps with phosphates, which cause algae growth that harms marine life, and avoid cleaners that release chlorine into the water and air. White vinegar can replace many common household cleaning products.

21. Watch for the "How's My Driving?" sticker and call trucking and cab companies whose vehicles spew black smoke to complain.

22. Avoid drive-throughs, warming up your car, talking in

your driveway with your car running, and other needless idling, which releases double the emissions of a moving car and adds to air and noise pollution.

23. Be an earth-smart driver. Keep your car tuned, tires properly inflated, and the air conditioner well maintained. Get service done only at repair facilities that recycle CFCs. Drive the speed limit and accelerate and slow down gradually.

24. Carpool or use public transportation when possible. Bike or walk for short trips.

25. When buying tee-shirts, choose ones made of *organic* cotton. Each regular, non-organic cotton tee takes 1/3 pound of pesticides to make. Or look for clothing made from wool, bamboo silk, switch grass, or recycled materials.

26. Avoid purchasing products that contain halocarbons (e.g. Halon fire extinguishers, aerosol cleaners for electronic or photographic equipment) and other ozone-destroying chemicals.

27. Whenever CFC-free refrigerators and automobile air conditioners are available, switch to these products.

28. Keep a travel mug in your car to fill up at the coffee shop or during meetings. Bring your own reusable bottle of cold water to outings and refill it as needed.

29. Start a compost pile in your yard.

30. Plant a tree and/or drought-resistant plants around your house.

31. Use organic pesticides and fertilizers.   Avoid using

chemical lawn products.

32. Start a community garden.

33. Enjoy family recreational activities that use sustainable rather than nonrenewable energy (e.g., hike instead of watching television).

34. Donate unwanted clothing and household items to charity or to a thrift shop.

35. Check with your local power company to see if they have green alternatives. If such a program is available, sign up for it. If not, ask them why.

36. Buy concentrated products. Look for at least 2x on the label. This saves packaging and energy to transport twice the amount of non-concentrated product. Also, buy in bulk or larger sizes and freeze or otherwise store in smaller, reusable containers.

37. Plan for leftovers. Cook double recipes and freeze half for a quick, easy second meal later. This uses less energy (PG&E and yours).

38. Go online to find eco-pocket guides, print them off and keep them with you while you shop. You can find ones on sustainable seafood, pesticides in products, household chemicals, personal products that contain unwanted chemicals, etc.

39. Free yourself from useless, wasteful bits of paper. Opt for paperless statements and bills and pay them online. Say "no" to receipts from ATM machines. Remove yourself from mailing lists you do not want to be on by contacting the offending companies. Get yourself off of junk mail lists and catalogs you don't read. Tell insurance and credit

card companies you don't want their offers.

40. Educate children about sustainable-living. Be a role-model for them.

A5. CHILDREN'S AGE-APPROPRIATE BOOKS

Through Grade 2

The Berenstain Bears Don't Pollute (Anymore), by Stan and Jan Berenstain.

Follow the Bear Country cubs as they learn about pollution, then watch them teach the adults around them.

Brother Eagle, Sister Sky: A Message from Chief Seattle, by Susan Jeffers.

Chief Seattle teaches the sacredness of the Earth itself and all of its inhabitants.

The Color of Us, by Karen Katz.

This book discusses the diversity of people and colors of skin and friendship among them.

Condor Magic, by Lyn Littlefield with illustrations by Peter Stone.

A story-in-rhyme of endangered California condors being saved and reintroduced into the wilds of Arizona.

Dinosaurs to the Rescue! A Guide to Protecting Our Planet, by Laurie Krasny Brown and Marc Brown.

Children learn how to conserve the Earth's resources (*Reduce*), find ways to reuse items we already have (*Reuse*), and what to do with no-longer-wanted items besides just throwing them in the trash (*Recycle*).

Eno's Garden, by Graeme Base.

Picture book about mistakes we make with our environment and what we can do to make those mistakes right. This is especially good for children who like counting games.

The Giving Tree, by Shel Silverstein.

An unselfish tree keeps giving to a child throughout his journey into adulthood, yet it asks nothing in return.

The Golden Rule, by Ilene Cooper and Gabi Swiatkowska.

This is a good one to read aloud to children. It focuses on the Golden Rule, with a young boy and his grandfather talking about how it can be found in all cultures and religions.

The Great Kapok Tree: A Tale of the Amazon Rain Forest, by Lynne Cherry.

A man comes to chop down the home of the animals living in a tree in the Brazilian rain forest and the inhabitants try to convince him to lay down his ax and not destroy it.

The Great Trash Bash, by Loreen Leedy.

Beaston has a huge trash problem. The animals who live there discover what they can do to solve it.

Hannah is My Name: A Young Immigrant's Story, by Belle Yang.

A young girl from China is waiting for her parents go get their green card.

It's Okay to Be Different, by Tom Parr.

People are all different. Some use wheelchairs or have big ears. It's okay to feel good about being different.

Just a Dream, by Chris Van Allsburg.

A dream about the future, when the Earth is severely damaged by pollution, changes the mind of a child who has been complaining about having to sort trash.

The Lorax, by Dr. Seuss.

Follow the greedy Once-ler as he destroys the wilderness homes of the creatures living there.

The Peace Book, by Tom Parr.

What is the meaning of Peace? A young child tells us his view.

Someday a Tree, by Eve Bunting and Ronald Himler.

Picture book about what happens to a single small part of the environment.

The Wartville Wizard, by Don Madden.

Litterbugs meet their match in a man who picks up bits of trash after people and sends it back to them.

Where Does the Garbage Go?, by Paul Showers.

This story answers the question about what happens after the truck picks up the abundance of waste people create.

Wolves in Yellowstone, by Randy Houk.

True story, told in rhyme, about how endangered gray wolves are returned to Yellowstone Park.

Grades 2 through 5

50 Simple Things Kids Can Do to Save the Earth, by John Javna.

Earth-saving tips for children, written at their level and designed as things they can do themselves.

Bus Station Mystery, by Gertrude Chandler Warner and David Cunningham.

Boxcar Children, caught in a bus station during a storm, end up in a mystery about a polluted river.

The Caped Sixth Grader: Totally Toxic, by Zoe Quinn and Brie Spangler.

A sixth grader who learns that the local river is being polluted by a company's dumping of wastes uses her superpowers to try to stop them.

Diary of a Worm, by Doreen Cronin.

Being a worm can be fun—and sometimes not so fun.

Earth Day, by Linda Lowery.

What does Earth Day have to do with children? This book explains how the day began and gives them some ideas about how they can participate in it.

The Everything Kids' Environment Book: Learn How You Can Help Save the Environment, by Sheri Arsel.

Kids learn how to get involved at school, at home, and while playing. Includes many engaging illustrations and puzzles.

Garbage Delight, by Dennis Lee.

This delightful book contains poems and drawings to illustrate where a variety of types of garbage comes from.

Going Green: A Kid's Handbook to Saving the Planet, by John Elkington, et al.

Children learn about the ecology and are given some projects they can do to help the environment.

Good Planets Are Hard to Find, by Roma Dehr and Ronald M. Bazar.

This book for older children in this age group teaches them how to protect the environment.

Keepers of the Earth: Native American Stories and Environmental Activities for Children, by Michael J. Caduto and Joseph Bruchac.

This is a collection of Native American tales that deal with the environment.

Let it Shine, by Andrea Davis Pinkney.

This is a good chapter book to read to younger children. It tells the stories of Sojourner

Truth and Shirley Chisholm and many other Black women freedom fighters in between.

Recycle! A Handbook for Kids, by Gail Gibbons.

Written for use by children, this book encourages them to recycle glass, paper, aluminum, polystyrene, and plastic and gives them ways to do so.

Trash!, by Charlotte Wilcox.

How is all that trash disposed of? Landfills, burning, and recycling are discussed.

Worms Eat My Garbage, by Mary Applehof.

Here's a fun project for children: worm composting. They learn what it is, how to do it, and what the end product can be used for.

Grades 4 through 6

Bud, Not Buddy, by Christopher Paul Curtis.

A young boy named Bud has lost his mother and is now running away.

Esperanza Rising, by Pam Munoz Ryan.

During the Depression, a woman is widowed and she takes her young daughter from Mexico to go to California to work in the fields.

Julian's Glorious Summer, by Ann Cameron.

All children face fears. In this story, a boy has a lie backfire on him.

Number the Stars, by Lois Lowry.

A young girl in Denmark during World War I helps her Jewish friend.

The Road to Paris, by Nikki Grimes.

Follow the life of Paris, a girl who is growing up in a series of foster homes.

Jackie O'Donnell

Grades 6 through 12

Call of the River, ed. by Page Stegner.

Beautiful photos, essays, and stories about rivers.

Carton, Cans and Orange Peels: Where Does Your Garbage Go?, by Joanna Foster.

What is all that garbage and what can be done with it? These questions are answered.

The Edge of the Sea, by Rachel Carson.

The environment discussed as only Rachel Carson can.

The Faces of Ceti, by Mary Caraker (novel).

Science fiction book about two groups of Earth settlers on nearby planets. One group builds its culture using force, while the other uses sound ecological judgments.

The Island, by Gary Paulsen.

Troubled by events at home, a 15-year-old goes to a near-by island and enjoys the nature around him.

The Kid's Guide to Social Action, by Barbara A. Lewis.

What can kids actually do to help save the Earth? Here they are told in easy-to-understand language.

Restoring the Earth: How Americans Are Working to Renew Our Damaged Environment, by John J. Berger.

Non-fiction book about various American conservationists.

Silent Spring, by Rachel Carson.

Rachael Carson's classic book that had a huge influence on how government looks at its responsibility and on the entire environmental movement.

The Throwaway Society, by Sally Lee.

More about the problem of disposing of garbage, written for young people to understand.

A6. ADULT BOOKS ON SOCIAL JUSTICE

Adventures in Simple Living: A Creation-Centered Spirituality, by Rich Heffern.

The assistant director of *Praying* magazine calls the reader to a richer life of simple, meaningful living to reap spiritual benefits. Time is money when you work for a living, and the less money you need the more time you have for meaningful living. Excerpts are included from ten years spent in the Ozarks on a small communal farm.

Beyond Guilt, by George S. Johnson.

Twenty-four sections of brief essays pose questions for developing social conscience.

Then, by using the author's excellent bibliography, the reader can research answers in greater depth. Johnson, a Lutheran pastor, asks the reader to celebrate God's goodness even in the face of suffering and to eliminate guilt by taking responsibility.

Bread for the World, by Arthur Simon.

The author, founding president of Bread For The World Foundation and a Lutheran minister, has served twenty years on New York's economically disadvantaged lower East side. He describes hunger, with both the social and economic causes, through a question/

answer format. Examples are portrayed in stories, graphics, and sidebars. The issues of population, resources, economics, and human rights are interwoven. U.S. policies play a key role.

Catholic Social Teaching, Our Best Kept Secret, by Edward P. DeBerri and James E. Hug.

Offers an overview of the history of the Catholic church's social teaching for students, teachers, and lay people as well as clergy. The authors present outlines of both recent and historic church documents to help Catholics appreciate and share their rich heritage of following Jesus' command to "love one another."

Compassion: A Reflection on the Christian Life, by Henri Nouwen, Donald P. McNeil, Douglas A. Morrison.

What is the meaning of "compassion," and what role does it play in our lives? The authors discuss the importance of compassionate love as an integral part of each Christian life.

Coyote Warrior: One Man, Three Tribes, and the Trial that Forged a Nation, by Paul VanDevelder.

How Martin Cross and three tribes fought the Federal government for their rights, survival, heritage, and dignity over a century and a half, as told through a family history.

Dead Man Walking, by Sister Helen Prejean.

A look at the death penalty through the relationship of a nun and a condemned man.

God's Politics: Why the Right gets it wrong, and the Left Doesn't get it, by Jim Wallis.

To come to grips with our nation's involvement in war, poverty, HIV/AIDS, abortion, capital punishment, plus issues of family and community value, we must examine the causes of these problems. The author challenges people of faith with a mandate to apply a guiding moral compass to these problems.

How Much is Enough?, by Arthur Simon.

How does our consumerist society fit in with our Christian calling?

Justice Prayer Book With Biblical Reflections, Faith and Human

Development Series, #5-231 (United States Catholic Conference).

In this collection of thoughts and meditations from spiritual leaders past and present, readers find guidance on how to more fully realize their identity as followers of Jesus through service to, advocacy for, and solidarity with the poor.

Meet Dorothy Day, Champion of the Poor, by Woodeene Koenig-Bricker.

Biography of Dorothy Day, giving insight on her life-journey from young, controversial journalist among Socialists and atheists, to dealing with her own spiritual confusion, to becoming an activist and founder of the Catholic Worker movement. Told through her own writings and words of people who knew her well.

Place at the Table—The Gay Individual in America, by BruceBawer.

An examination of the gay-rights movement, stereotypes, and what fosters fear and hostility against gays and lesbians. The author shows the diversity of beliefs, politics, and values that make up the homosexual population.

Reading Lolita in Tehran, by Azar Nafisi.

Picture of women's lives in Iran under strict religious rule. Individual personalities and difficult personal decisions are shown as a group of women meet secretly to discuss novels.

Red Sky at Morning: America and the Crisis of the Global Environment (A Citizen's Agenda for Action), by James Gustave Speth.

An examination of the world's environment and America's role in preserving it.

Rich Christians in an Age of Hunger: Moving from Affluence to Generosity, by Ronald J. Sider.

What is poverty? What does the Bible say about the poor? What causes poverty? How can we as individuals and a nation work toward a more fair world? In this book, the author tries to get readers to think seriously about these questions, and he gives specific answers to them.

Saint Francis and the Foolishness of God, by Marie Dennis, et al.

A collection of biographies of St. Francis of Assisi. The authors, Catholic and Protestant, present St. Francis as he struggles with poverty, violence, and suffering. The reader sees both his human and his spiritual sides.

Send My Roots Rain: A Spirituality of Justice and Mercy, by Megan McKenna.

The author, a scholar, teacher, speaker and retreat leader, presents parables—stories of love, freedom, peace, friendship and loss—which show fulfillment through mercy and justice. The stories range from sad to humorous, but all are very human.

Simple life: Plain Living and High Thinking in American Culture, by David E. Shi.

The author writes about the importance of making the decision to live a simpler life, then doing it and the resultant improved spiritual health of the individual and moral health of the nation.

Simpler Living, Compassionate Life: a Christian Perspective, by Henri Nouwen, R. Foster, et al.

The articles in this book question what the "good life" is and focus readers on improving our lives through simplicity. Discussions cover major aspects of daily life, such as food, money, time, spirituality, heritage, and community.

Stormy Weather: 101 Solutions to Global Climate Change, by Guy Dauncey, with Patrick Mazza.

Presents solutions to offset climate changes in the world and prevent further ones.

'Tis a Gift to be Simple, by Barbara DeGrote-Sorensen and David DeGrote-Sorense.

More than slowing down, a life style of simplicity makes an important statement to the world family. Voluntary simplicity is a matter of obedience, living faith integrated with life, a personal commitment to a more equitable distribution of the world's resources. This book offers a biblical and spiritual foundation for making changes that reflect God's priorities in our lives.

Toward A Spirituality For Global Justice: A Call to Kinship, by Elaine Prevalett.

The author broadens our sense of justice to include kinship with all members of the community of Earth and living a life of commitment and compassion. Viewing life's possibilities through a threefold lens of science, the solidarity of humanity, and a vision of communion, the author explores the riches of the Hebrew Scriptures and the treasures of the Christian Gospel, opening new insights for her readers and relating them to present times.

The Weather Makers, by Tim Flannery.

It is urgent that we address *now* the implications of a global climate change that is damaging all life on earth and endangering our very survival. This book is unimpeachable in its authority and deftly and accessibly written, giving us a vision for what each of us can do to avoid catastrophe. The author reminds us that we already possess the tools required to avoid catastrophic climate change.

Word of God, the Word of Peace, by Patricia McCarthy, C.N.D.

Using Scripture, Sr. McCarthy explains God's process of peace and justice, from His request, to our response, to what is required of us, to the rewards. She quotes passages from the Old and New Testaments to explain each part of the process. (This book can be read alone or as part of the Little Rock Scripture Study on "The Way of Justice and Peace.")

Why Do They Hate Me? Young Lives Caught in War and Conflict, by Laurel Holliday.

Portions of diaries and journals written by children and teenagers as they lived through the Holocaust and WW II, The Troubles in Northern Ireland, and the Israeli/Palestinian conflict.

The Tortilla Curtain, by T.C. Boyle (novel).

A young Mexican brings his pregnant wife to Southern California so he can work and provide a better life for them. He is hit by the car of a local resident who prides himself on his liberal attitudes but lives in an exclusive community which is drawing more inward. The book, which follows the lives of these people as they cross again and again, shows how influences can change attitudes—not always for the better.

The Irresistible Revolution: Living As an Ordinary Radical, by Shane Claiborne.

The author believes in love within us being put into action in the broken world around us. He invites people to follow his example of action, from working with Mother Teresa and helping lepers, dumping $10,000 onto Wall Street to make a point about redistributing wealth, or simply living among the local poor and helping local children.

The Faith That Does Justice: Examining the Christian Source for Social Change, ed. by John Haughey.

A very useful collection of essays by scholars such as Avery Dulles, John Donahue, John Langan,Jr., David Hollenbach, and John Haughley.

Fullness of Faith, by Michael and Kenneth Himes.

An insightful work that provides theological reflection on Catholic social thought and public theology. Notable chapters include "Original Sin," "The Trinity and Human Rights," "Grace and a Consistent Ethic of Life," and "The Communion of Saints and an Ethic of Solidarity."

American Strategic Theology, by John A. Coleman.

The author shows how the Christian Gospel fits into contemporary American culture. The book presents the church as a sacrament to the world, as a community that is gathered precisely for the purpose of being sent into the world.

The Moral Core of Judaism and Christianity, by Daniel C. Maguire.

A powerful and bold attempt to refute the myth that there is no commonality in the Jewish and Christian traditions of moral thought. The theme of justice is prominent in this work. It provides a good opportunity to better understand social teaching in the wider context of Judeo Christian thought.

Ownership - Early Christian Teaching, by Charles Avila.

An anthology of early Christian teachings on the theme of ownership. Writers in the third and fourth centuries had a surprisingly radical and consistent tradition of thought on ownership and property. Works of Clement of Alexandria, Basil the Great, Ambrose, John Chrysostom and Augustine are among those included.

Let Justice Roll Down Like Waters, by Walter J. Burghardt, S.J.

A collection of homilies by one of the Catholic Church's best preachers. The focus is on biblical justice, and the homilies cover a wide range of dates within the liturgical year as well as special events.

Following Christ in a Consumer Society, by John F. Kavanaugh.

Examines Christian values and how they can be lived in our modern society.

❧ *Appendix B*

If you want to reread an article but can't remember where it is, this Appendix will help. It will also direct you to that helpful list or set of instructions you saw. For your convenience, the titles or topics are in alphabetical order and each is followed by the number of the specific chapter in which you can find it.

B1. ARTICLES

Animal Experimentation: *If it makes products safer, why not?* (chapter 8)

Beat the System—Volunteer: *Make a difference by getting involved* (chapter 2)

Be Aware: *Notice the opportunities around us each day* (chapter 10)

Be Heard! *The power of our stated opinion* (chapter 2)

Budgets: *Budgeting as though we believe in God* (chapter 10)

Burger Boy: *Thoughts of a low-wage fast-food worker* (chapter

3)

Celebrate Peace: *Observe September 21 's annual U.N. International Day of Peace (chapter 9)*

Charity on a Budget: *How to find money that you can share with others* (chapter 4)

Chill Out: *Begin the peace process by making peace with your own life (chapter 9)*

Christmas (A New Tradition): *An idea for a new holiday tradition for your family* (chapter 11)

Classic Films: *Classic movies can make us think* (chapter 10)

Click Away Hunger: *While you're checking your email, sign on to a site that donates food for every click you make* (chapter 3)

Closed-Wallet Giving: *Ways to give without even opening your wallet* (chapter 4)

Couples TV Dinner: *Gather in front of the TV with friends for a meal, a video, and some talk* (chapter 5)

Day Workers: *Improve a life and your house at the same time* (chapter 3)

Don't Just Stand There! *A child tells her story of a frightening experience and who was there to help* (chapter 2)

Dumb Blonde: *Jokes that reveal our attitudes* (chapter 7)

Easter: *The season is longer than a single day* (chapter 11)

Earthly Considerations: *A common-sense approach to the global-*

landfill (chapter 8)

Room for God: *Set aside space for God to fill with His love* (chapter 4)

Rotating Shelter: *Small ways to support a worthwhile Program* (chapter 4)

Safe Haven: *Protect children in the neighborhood* (chapter 5)

Safety First! *Help provide a safer home for all your neighbors* (chapter 4)

Servers: *Honor food servers* (chapter 3)

Share a Hobby: *Brighten someone else's life while you enjoy your Hobby* (chapter 4)

Shop for Causes: *Something you plan to buy can help others* (chapter 2)

Signing Petitions: *Be careful what you wish for* (chapter 10)

Sign of Peace: *It's more than just a ritual* (chapter 9)

Speak English: *How dare those people in line with us talk to each other in another language!* (chapter 6)

Sticks and Stones: *That old children's chant is more hurtful than we want to admit* (chapter 7)

Strange People: *They're all us around, but who are they?* (chapter 7)

Take Jesus to Work Day: *If there's a Take Your Child to Work Day, why not one for Jesus?* (chapter 10)

Teach Charity: *Teaching our children simples acts of charity*

B2. LISTS AND INSTRUCTIONS

Printed in the United States
215330BV00002B/2/P

9 781926 625232